CAN YOU MAKE
THE BUTTONS EVEN?

LESSONS LEARNED ALONG LIFE'S
SPIRITUAL PATH

BY

Richard C. Cheatham

Bloomington, IN Milton Keynes, UK

authorHOUSE

AuthorHouse™
1663 Liberty Drive, Suite 200
Bloomington, IN 47403
www.authorhouse.com
Phone: 1-800-839-8640

AuthorHouse™ UK Ltd.
500 Avebury Boulevard
Central Milton Keynes, MK9 2BE
www.authorhouse.co.uk
Phone: 08001974150

First published by AuthorHouse 5/11/2006

ISBN: 1-4259-2102-7 (sc)

Library of Congress Control Number: 2006902016

Printed in the United States of America
Bloomington, Indiana

This book is printed on acid-free paper.

Cover Design by Wendy Schleicher
Cover Photo by Dr. Cynthia Beamer

TABLE OF CONTENTS

MEANING WAS UNDERSTOOD. IT CALLS FOR A RADICAL RETHINK-
ING OF THE GOOD NEWS.

ACKNOWLEDGEMENTS

I must thank those faithful students at the Franklin Community, Birmingham First, and University United Methodist Churches in Michigan and San Antonio who worked with me during the developmental stages of this book. Their questions, reactions, proofreading and encouragement were vital to bringing the manuscript to fruition. There are some I would like to acknowledge more specifically. I fear, however, that I might inadvertently omit some if I were to try. So let me merely offer a special thanks to those of you who went that extra mile in proofreading, in contributing your thoughts, and in offering your encouragement.

I have drawn from my daughters, Debbie Exe, Cindy Beamer, and Crystal Myers, throughout the book. Sometimes obviously - sometimes anonymously - sometimes from the experiences which shaped my understanding. It has been said that our parents can only raise us to a certain point of maturity. Then it is our children who cause us to grow up. In my case, at least, that has been true. Their interest and encouragement in this endeavor also has been very important and very dear to me.

My wife, Diane, undoubtedly is the reason the book has found its way to completion and into print. She has believed in me and this work - probably far more than I. Without her patient and careful reading and rereading, her gentle (and sometimes not-so-gentle) prodding me toward completion much of what has been written would still be lying around in my head somewhere.

Finally, I think of the words from Tennyson's *Ulysses*, "I am a part of all that I have met . . ." There are so many persons who have served as guides and teachers along my spiritual path. They have offered words of encouragement during difficult times; expressed reactions to things I said; shared private thoughts in quiet moments; and have made candid observations of life. Sometime it was an honest confrontation on significant issues. Perhaps more often it was a simple case of osmosis - a slow interchange of understanding which occurs over time with friends. The people of the Napoleon United Methodist Church, where I served as a student pastor, have a special place in my heart. They embraced an inexperienced, young pastor, bore with his mistakes and loved him and his family on their way. Many of the people at my other Michigan United Methodist congregations: Glacier Way, St. James, Brighton, and Franklin also are very much a part of who I am. We learn from experience and from example - much good - some bad . . . some questionable. To continue with Tennyson's words: ". . . yet all experience is an arch wherethro' gleams that untravell'd world whose margin fades forever and forever as I move."

PREFACE

Why one more book on spirituality? Judging from the titles I see at the local book venders one would imagine there already is a surfeit on the subject, and another would be as welcome as a leaky faucet in a flood. Still I believe there is an area which has yet to be fully explored. The term *spirituality* is a multifaceted word. I know of spirituality workshops where the main emphasis is upon prayer. I've seen others which focus upon an inner knowing of the self. Some use biblical phrases in their attempt to develop personal traits which have come under the heading of spiritual gifts. If you ask someone what they intend to acquire in any spirituality workshop I would guess that their response would be, at best, vague. It is my belief that our true spirituality is worked out in the market place, the living room, the bedroom, the kitchen, the highways and by-ways, the classrooms, the playgrounds and all the other hallways of life. The church may serve as our guide through these personal labyrinths. Still our spiritual pilgrimage is distinctively our own, and it is the meat and potatoes of our life. It is the very stuff which determines what we ultimately call "character." Our spirituality - for better or for worse - determines what kind of person we become, whatever meaning we find in living, and what we leave behind as a witness that we once walked this sacred earth.

It is a life-long pilgrimage. There is no easy twelve step process or thirty day "fix." These may give surges of spiritual adrenaline, but they are reminiscent of Jesus' warnings of the seeds which sprouted quickly but had no roots (Matthew 13:5-6). The reader will have to be patient. It *is* a life-long pilgrimage. There is no point at which one may say, "I have arrived!" There are only resting places where one may look back and realize, with satisfaction perhaps, how far one has journeyed. The Swiss psychologist, Carl Jung, cautioned that the mind is the logos portion of our being. It quickly grasps the truths presented and embraces them. However the soul is the agricultural portion of our being which grows and heals slowly.

There is, of course, a second dimension to the spiritual quest, equally significant . . . perhaps even more so. It is hinted at in Acts 17:28, when Paul speaks of God in this manner:

For in Him we live and move and have our being.

As surely as there is a physical realm of existence, there is also a spiritual. Our creeds state it: "God is Omnipresent." This does not suggest some super Being who is everywhere at once. Rather, it speaks of an all-pervading Spirit in which "we live and move and have our being." The second dimension of the spiritual quest is to live as fully in that realm as we do in the physical. This, I believe, is the lesson Jesus Christ taught by his words, his actions, and his death and resurrection. It was what he meant when he said, "I am the way, the truth and the life." (John 14:6) Our personal spiritual pilgrimage necessarily leads us in that way. It is when we reside in that realm - even partially - that we experience God's Presence, that we gain fresh awareness of the sacredness of all of life, and that we discover powers of understanding and - yes, even powers of healing - which normally evade us.

Some acquire this quality of spiritual life more readily than others. There *are* varying gifts of the spirit. Still, to have been made in God's image is to possess - or to be endowed with - some potential of profound spirituality . . . of dwelling in the Realm of Spirit. This is the end toward which all of life moves. The earth is but a temporary dwelling place. The Realm of the Spirit is our ultimate home.

These excerpts from my own spiritual pilgrimage reflect these two aspects of spirituality. As an ordained clergyperson, I have blended my educational tools with my personal experiences to guide me through some of the spiritual passages of my journey. These are not the only resources, however. There are spiritual dimensions available to seekers which guide and empower us as we go. I shall share them, as appropriate, as I relate some of my lessons learned along life's spiritual path. Each lesson required years to complete and mature into a higher stage. I share them because I believe all personal experiences - although unique in and of themselves - have some common ground to which others can relate and understand. In the sharing and the understanding I hope that my struggles may assist and encourage you in yours.

I have selected from a variety of translations, e.g. NIV, RSV, NSRV. In some instances I have made my own from the Greek or altered one of the above, selecting a word I believed more nearly expressed the meaning of the original Greek. For example, in most cases when the term "men" is used it is *anthropos* which means humans rather than males. Also, in many cases when the translators use the term "he" the actual Greek more appropriately would be neuter as in II Corinthians 5:17: "If any person is in Christ that one is a new creation," not "*he* is a new creation." Similarly, the Greek term *telos* depicts completion, fulfillment, or maturity, yet translators tend to use "perfect" which I believe carries a connotation which often alters the true meaning of many phrases. In any case the variety of translations may help the reader to understand that there is no one clear word, and each of us ultimately is called upon, as Paul says, to work out our own salvation in fear and in trembling. (Philippians 2:12)

I have altered the names of those I mention in order to protect their privacy.

INTRODUCTION

Each of us is on a spiritual pilgrimage, *whether we know it or not.* We are not mere physical creatures who occasionally have a spiritual experience. We are *spiritual beings* who are presently undergoing a physical experience. Life itself is a journey from infancy to eternity. Once we realize this we are able to give our lives depth and direction. Until we understand this we are apt to spend much of our time roaming in the wilderness or merely straying through life . . . without any realization that we have lost our way. The two principal questions we should ask about life are "What are we to do with the time given us?" and "In what condition are we to arrive in eternity when this earthly life has run its course?" We are called to make the living worth while in a manner which moves us in a direction that draws us ever closer to God.

The Book of Genesis offers two creation stories. Both attempt to make a statement about Creation and humanity. Both have a message that is significant for the spiritual pilgrim. They are blended together so that the casual reader seldom notices the blending of two diverse tales. The first affirms the goodness of the entire Creation (Genesis 1:1-2:3). There is no Garden of Eden. Humanity is made in the image of God and given dominion over the earth. The second is more primitive (Genesis 2:4-3:24). The male is created first, constructed of clay and set in the Garden of Eden. The female is constructed from his rib and joins him in the garden. They are innocent and dependent. When they disobey God by eating fruit from the tree of awareness, they become self-conscious and are forced to leave the garden and toil the earth as punishment. If the reader understands the purpose of myth, both of these stories tell important truths. Every culture has its myths, or stories, which tell of the origin of things. Truly worthy myths have something of the quality of the parables conceived by Jesus. His parable of the Prodigal Son, for example, was a statement about the forgiving nature of God. Myths are not necessarily factual, but they serve to present a truth which is too large to be explained in ordinary prose. The two myths of Creation in Genesis have prevailed through the centuries because they speak of universal truths. The first affirms the essential goodness of Creation and humanity. The second tells of *The Fall* which each of us experiences as we mature. Within the individual soul it echoes our loss of innocence and sense of being orphaned in the world The Eden story does not speak of an original sin that is transmitted from generation to generation. Neither does it lessen the understanding of the first story which affirms that humanity is made in the image of God and is essentially good.

It is this essential goodness which I affirm and use as part of my spiritual pilgrimage.

In extreme instances Christian theology has twisted the Genesis story to claim the total depravity of humanity. In far too many instances it has twisted the story just enough to generate a sense of perpetual guilt in its adherents. Christian liturgies and hymnals are filled with references to our unworthiness and need for redemption. They suggest we are dependent and incapable of rising above our sinful nature on our own. While sins of commission and omission, and their accompanying guilt are realities of life, they are not the *core* realities, which the church should be addressing. The more basic and vital issues are what is termed *ontological guilt* and the underlying cause of those sins of commission and omission.

Ontological guilt deals with our sense of being and becoming. We are not accidents of an impersonal nature. Each of us has been created by a loving God for a purpose. We are called to become someone in particular in this lifetime. In the early portion of life we are simply trying to understand the rules by which we are to live. As time progresses we begin to focus on the purpose of that living. We establish goals and we set priorities. Usually these reflect the goals and priorities of those important to us at the time. Our parents, mentors, and peer groups guide us by placing boundaries and by rewarding us in various ways for accepting their values. We become *accepted, praised,* or *loved.* Our own experience and character, however, play a role in this early development.

Somewhere along life's journey we begin to sense a call to become more than we are. This may arise as a sense of dissatisfaction with some portion of our lives. It may come as a spiritual awakening. It may arrive through a series of events which appear rather ordinary, but ultimately result in our setting some new goals and/or rearranging our life priorities.

Each of us is unique. Our thoughts and reactions may follow a pattern. Still, we are not manufactured copies of one another. We have a vast assortment of unique, personal gifts placed within the hidden recesses of our souls. We are not blank sheets of humanity with our scripts written by others. In the final analysis we write our own story. We shape our own lives and destinies within the limitations and possibilities given us by the arena in which our lives are acted. However, in this regard we are not left without guidance. Christians call this guidance the Holy Spirit. Doors of our lives and our minds are silently opened and closed to guide us on our way if we are attentive to them.

We also are given some kind of outline as a guide for writing and living that story. Christians call this *Holy Scripture.* Even here, however, it becomes personal and unique. We each have our own collection of Scriptures from which we shape our faith and our lives. There are passages which have jumped from the pages into our souls, proclaiming, "Yes! This is true! This is what life is about!" There are countless others we have simply passed over and forgotten. They did not resonate within us, or did not fit into the pattern which was forming in our lives. Hopefully our personal collection increases through the years as life adds depth and direction to our being. It is these words which are often summoned into our consciousness in times of crises to remind of who we are, *whose* we are, and where we are headed.

As a part of this book I have assembled a few passages which have been fundamental in shaping my faith as it has developed thus far. I place them in context, sharing - in so far as possible - the events, feelings and thoughts which gave them meaning. I share them because I believe they are reflective of experiences which have enough commonality to speak to you. Sometimes the passages helped to shape the experience. Sometimes they aided in the understanding. Sometimes they became meaningful for me in retrospect, and joined my ongoing collection which helps to guide and shape future events.

These are excerpts from my personal spiritual diary. They represent a few of the hard-learned lessons of life. To be sure, there are far more than the few I shall mention in this writing. I selected these because I believe they are basic to all of us. Each has been significant to my personal pilgrimage and may serve as a guide for your own journey.

1. LET GO OF YOUR LITTLE GOD

We had just completed evening chapel service and she came to me with a serious look on her young face. " I need to talk with you," she said with the earnest tones of a young teenager wrestling with a major problem. I nodded and waited, then she continued. "You see, I don't think I believe in God anymore." She uttered this with an almost apologetic tone to me, and I could see she was hoping this would not affect our relationship. She knew she was one of my favorites at camp, so she trusted me enough to tell me of her growing agnosticism. I had watched her through four years of choir camp, as she grew from a cute little eleven year old to a bright, talented, and disciplined fourteen year old high school freshman teeming with life and enthusiasm.

"What's happened?" I asked simply. Then we walked together over to the base of the flag pole, seated ourselves on it, and looked over the now quiet waters of Lake Huron.

"I've always believed in God and what the Bible told us about Him. I pray regularly and try to do what He wants." She paused, then continued: "I've never asked anything for myself . . . until my grandfather got sick. Then I prayed for him. I prayed he would get well . . . but he didn't." The memory was causing tears to form, almost invisibly, in her eyes. "Then I prayed that he would die peacefully and quickly . . . and not have to suffer much." Now she was having difficulty in speaking, and her pain became so intense that I could feel it with her. She paused for a moment to compose herself, then continued. "Why would God do that to him?" She had finally blurted it out, partly in sorrow, partly in anger.

1

I did not attempt to answer. Forget eight years of seminary! There simply is no theological response for such a question. It is not a question of the head. It is a cry of the heart.

In the silence my mind relived such moments.

In my first parish there was a saintly, retired clergyman: slender, dignified, essentially blind, but possessed of a beautiful spirit which overflowed through a keen mind into marvelous moments of wisdom. I recalled visiting him in the hospital as he was in the process of dying from a massive stroke. He sat diapered, strapped into a hospital bed, unseeing, unknowing . . . waiting for the moment of release. Later, his lovely widow asked me simply, "Why?" I was in seminary at the time, freshly filled with all the knowledge that could be packed into my head. But I just shook my head slowly and replied, "I don't know . . . . I don't know."

For all the "Whys" which have followed during forty years of ministry - and there have been far too many - I have never attempted to articulate an answer. Still those moments have never shaken my basic faith in God. Each has caused me to let go of some cherished image of God and reshape - and reshape again - my understanding of this God of Abraham, Isaac, Jacob, and Jesus Christ, who in some undeniable manner lays claim to every fiber of my being and every dimension of my soul.

She had begun to speak again, and I had to struggle to pull my attention back to the present - and to her. She was saying something to the effect that she could not believe in, or like, a God who would do that to her grandfather. I inwardly winced, recalling how I had been angry at God when my mother died. I had not been able to understand why she who was so full of life had to die, while a miserable, passive-dependant member of my congregation continued to live her wretched existence.

She paused, waiting for some kind of response from me. She had told her story. Now she wanted some help, or at least an acknowledgement that I understood and accepted her. I looked into her serious, young

2

face. Behind us many of the campers were playing, laughing, hand-holding, and generally going about their business of being carefree and young. "Why her?" I thought. She was far too young to begin such an important pilgrimage. She ought to be out there with the others, enjoying herself lightheartedly. I realized, however, that this young lady always was a bit ahead of her time.

At length I replied, slowly and gently "You have started your pilgrimage," Then I waited for her reaction.

She did not disappoint me. "What do you mean, "a pilgrimage?'" she asked intently.

"You are letting go of the God of your childhood, and are beginning a search for a God who is large enough, complex enough, and powerful enough to be the God you will love and serve as an adult."

We sat in silence as she processed this thought, both of us watching the slow roll of waves upon the beach. Finally it was *my* turn to break the silence. "The God presented to you as a child was all you needed while you were a child and your world was simple. Your world no longer is simple enough for that little god, so you must either let him go or try to go back and recreate a simple world for yourself."

She sat quietly and waited until the shadows began to lengthen on the beach. I continued, "You *could* recreate that simple world, you know. Some people do it for themselves. They answer all the God questions by claiming a lack of faith for other people, or God's punishment or judgment . . . or simply with the tidy slogan, 'God has His reasons.' Then they accept situations which should be explored and possibly changed . . . or at least acknowledged and mourned."

Now she was into the discussions and not about to let me off the hook simply by blowing her God away with my words. "But how can you love a God who would do such things?"

"I could not! I did not! I did the same thing you are doing. I was quite a bit older, however. I had returned from Korea neither liking

3

nor believing in God - for all your reasons and more." My mind slid back to my own era of disbelief and anger at a God - and a world - that could produce such cruelty. "That is when I began *my* pilgrimage. It took years to arrive at the point where I even *wanted* to believe - or *could* believe in a Presence and a Power who was in some way responsible for this world. No one could give me this God. I had to discover Him for myself, precisely as you must. Even then you will be forever defining and redefining your image with every new crisis, every new sorrow, every new event which challenges your old understanding."

She sat quietly taking in my words. Her face had become even more serious, and I could see that she was beginning to realize the magnitude of what was taking place within her soul. I wanted to lighten and affirm the moment so I broke the silence. "There is some part of me that celebrates this moment with you, my little agnostic." She looked puzzled, and also relieved that I had changed the tone of our discussion. Her eyes danced, and asked the question without the necessity of words. I nodded.

"Like Abraham in the desert . . . ..

Like Moses scaling Mt. Sinai . . . ..

Like Jesus fasting in the wilderness . . . ..

Like Galahad venturing in search for the Holy Grail . . . ..

You are undertaking the most important - the most rewarding - journey of your life. *You are beginning the quest for God!* Forget what has happened earlier. Then you were being taught *about* God. Then you were being given a god who came at you from out of the past: From biblical passages, or from someone else's experience. These were valuable understandings, but they were incomplete fragments of the God of Jesus Christ."

We stared at one another in silence for a moment. I waited . . . .. It was now her turn to speak. She waited . . . then nodded. Our conversation was at its end. As we walked back to where it was we were

4

going I told her to find some guide or guides she trusted. Then I assured her I would be willing to listen if she ever wanted to call me.

I continue to hold her in my prayers, as I hold so many pilgrim friends in special prayers. If we are fortunate we eventually arrive at some point where we simply must let go of the little god of our childhood and begin the quest for what Paul Tillich once called, "The God beyond God." We simply cannot go through life ignoring the inequities. We cannot consider ourselves specially chosen and blessed by God because we happened to be born where there is fertile land, highly developed technology, advanced medical and health care, extraordinary freedom, and opportunity to attain "the good life." We cannot claim a belief in a just and loving God who watches over *all* His children, and then easily dismiss the terrible irony that half the world is hungering for food while our nation suffers from a variety of eating disorders related to a wasteful abundance of food.

We cannot dismiss the senseless tragedies that destroy lives, and not inquire about God's role in our lives . . . if we really believe in God.

The story is told of a man whose car was totally destroyed in an accident. It took hours for the rescue workers to cut him loose from the wreckage. When at last he was freed, he surveyed the mass of twisted metal which had nearly taken his life. Then he remarked, "Somebody up there must like me." One of the weary workers replied, "Either that, or somebody up there doesn't *want* you."

Far too many people who profess a belief in God actually have a little, personal god whose primary task is to watch over them. Early in my professional ministry I chanced upon a book by J.B. Phillips entitled, *Your God is Too Small.* He wrote of the "God in a Box" who was available on call, but safely tucked away when it was inconvenient to have God around.

I am reminded of the story of an elderly gentleman who had been non-religious for most of his life. However, on his seventieth birthday he began attending church regularly. When asked why he had done this, he explained that when he arrived at the gates of Heaven he wanted God to be able to recognize him. This may cause a chuckle among some, but I wonder at the strange, little god he must have had. He envisioned one who essentially was confined to church worship services - one who could be deceived by appearances - one who could be manipulated to reward him for his hypocrisy.

Many people have a tiny god who is more like an indulgent uncle. He does not take sin seriously. Rather, he pats them on the head and says, "I know how it is, but try to do better in the future, will you?" I do not believe this works in real life. I look about me and see a world that produces dreadful consequences for errors of omission and commission:

Pilot error and 200 people die a fiery death.

Something dreadfully wrong occurs in a family and five children are drowned.

A careless smoker destroys thousands of acres of forest.

Another falls asleep and perishes as a flaming torch.

One person breaks a vow and an entire family is shattered.

A public figure trades his integrity for gain and a career is ruined.

I do not see easy forgiveness or inconsequential punishments for our misdeeds when I look about me in the everyday world. To be sure, we all have made foolish mistakes while driving and have escaped accidents. *All* errors, *all* violations of ethics are not immediately and drastically punished. We may attribute this to grace or good fortune. However, we cannot speak of a God who does not care what we do, or dismisses any consequences. If we interpret "God will take care of me" to make God into some personal good luck charm, then what becomes of our faith when we draw our last breath, as some day we must?

"Curse God and die," Job's wife pleaded. His protection and blessing had failed them, and she was without hope. In the modern version of the story, *J.B.* by Archibald MacLeish, J.B. equates God to good fortune and *knows* he is blessed with it. Later, as the ills pile up, a character opines, "If God is good He isn't God. If God is God He isn't good." When God is perceived to be some celestial puppet master who controls every string, every facet of life, then the reflective person must honestly conclude that God is not good.

This is precisely the issue with which my young camper friend was wrestling, was it not? If God is the loving magician who causes everything to happen at His will, yet refuses to answer her prayers or ease her grandfather's pain, then something is terribly wrong.

Having studied our two thousand years of church history, I have come to the conclusion that most people do their theology backwards. They begin with some preconceived conception of God. It probably is a composite of popular religion, nationalism, political affiliation, cultural philosophy, prevailing morals, and some biblical images taken out of context (possibly from some bad Hollywood film). Next they attempt to fit Jesus Christ into their equation.

(I have long asserted that, in the beginning God created humanity in His image . . . and since that time humanity has been returning the favor).

When Moses encountered God in the burning bush on that Midian hillside, he wanted to learn His name. To possess the name of a deity was to be able to exercise some control over that deity. The name God gave to him was YHWH, which best translates as "I AM" or "I will be who I will be." (Exodus 3:14). An infinite God is more than a human mind can comprehend. An infinite God is beyond human control. An infinite God will be what He will be, and will do what He will do. An infinite God is beyond our language's ability to express: more than a *He* or a *She,* or a combination of both. Jesus gave us the term "Father" to denote a filial, loving relationship with the One who is the ultimate authority of our lives. In the Garden of Gethsemane he prayed to God to "remove this cup from me." But then he added, "Yet not what I want, but what you want." (Mark 14:36). Even the Christ of God acknowledged the ultimate authority and will of God.

To define God for human comprehension, Jesus once said, "He who has seen me has seen the Father.." (John 14:9) When he said "No one comes to the Father except through me" (John 14:6) he certainly did not mean that if you attend church regularly and assume the name of Christian God will accept you. What he meant was that one can only approach God in understanding by comprehending the mind and spirit of Jesus. Jesus as the anointed one of God is the clearest focus of the very nature of God and the means of access to become a member of God's spiritual family.

There is a point at which we no longer can cling to the God of our childhood and live with integrity. We must stand with the writer of the 8th Psalm and utter in awe, "My God, My God, how majestic is your name in all the earth. When I consider the moon and the stars which you have ordained, what are we that you are mindful of us." We must recognize that we do not create a god for our purpose. Rather it is *we* who have been - and still are being - created by God for *God's* purpose.

We may fill our lives with various diversions to keep ourselves busy and amused. However, if we fail to become whatever it is that God calls us to become our lives will not hold together.

If we fail to understand God's will, and violate that will - even with good intentions - our souls will never know the light.

If we serve the wrong god and are led toward oblivion - the brokenness of our spirits will remain unhealed.

If we simply choose to ignore God and live as though God does not exist, the contradictions of our lives will never give us peace.

The one who calls us to obedience and a cross also is the one who assures us that we who are weary and heavily laden may come and find rest.

The one who wept at the death of his friend Lazarus also is the one who stood at the entrance of his tomb and called him forth again into life.

The one who spilled his blood for us on the cross also is the one who called out from that cross for our forgiveness.

There is no God we are capable of creating - or imagining - or even fully comprehending - who can answer all the questions of life - ease the pains - solve all the problems - fulfill all our dreams.

There are moments when understanding simply is not enough.

When there are no answers . . .

When there are no words . . .

When there is no balm in Gilead to heal the sin-sick soul, mend the broken heart, make sense of chaos, or calm the inner terror . . .

There are moments when there is only God, and God's Presence to hold us together, comfort, sustain and renew us - and point our feet toward tomorrow.

Faith alone can reveal that God in the moments of crisis.

Faith alone can draw us into a relationship of understanding and trust.

Without this faith we fall into the abyss . . . in fear and in trembling.

With this faith we are empowered to leap into the darkness in certainty that underneath are the everlasting arms, and we shall not be left to fall throughout all eternity.

Faith which sustains like this is born of obedience to the commands of the Man of Galilee, who calls us from our little ledges of security to continue in his way through the darkness and the dawns of uncertainty, in humble service to others in His name.

He calls us to give of ourselves in order to find more than ourselves.

There comes to every one of us the moment to decide whether we wish to continue living our lives centered on ourselves and a little god of our own making, or whether we are willing to let go of our little god, and allow the God of Creation - the God of Jesus Christ - to lay claim upon us. Paul's admonition to the Philippians echoes somewhere within my soul: "*. . . not only in my presence, but more in my absence, work out your own salvation in fear and in trembling, for God is at work in you, both to will and to work for his good pleasure.*" (Phil. 2: 12)

REFLECTIONS

There is some inner portion of ourselves that is a seeker. It remains dormant until spurred into action, seeking to find something which has been lost. It may be some cherished belief which has given us a sense of comfort and/or security. It may be a broken relationship, a vanished dream, or a host of other possibilities, which thrust us from our personal Eden. Even then, only the emotionally secure will venture forth. Seeking requires courage. Those who lack that courage will bewail their loss and wait for rescue. They will become frozen in time, looking for a way back which does not exist. The great heroes of the faith have been willing to leave whatever constituted security for them, in order to become the persons God intended them to be. The God of the 20th and 21st centuries is too large to be contained by any literal interpretation of Scripture. In a universe which extends more than twelve billion light years in space there can be no "man upstairs." The writer of Psalm 139 had a grasp of that reality when he wrote:

Whether shall I go from thy spirit? Or whether shall I flee from thy presence? If I ascend into heaven thou art there. If I descend into Sheol thou art there.

(Psalm 139:7-8)

Omnipresent does not suggest a person who gets around quickly. Rather it describes a spirit which pervades Creation, as Jesus, himself, stated in John 4:24: *"God is Spirit, and those who worship him must worship in spirit and in truth."* While we might all wish to have a genii in a bottle to do our bidding, the God of Creation is not one that upsets the laws of nature for our personal benefit. The Innocent Child which lives within each of us longs for a genii or fairy godmother who will watch over us and protect us. When the magic or the religious faith fails to safeguard us and our loved one, we either must rethink or redesign the system. Many Innocents, in order to maintain their innocence, and accompanying feelings of security, begin a never-ending process of rationalization. It requires courage to face reality. It also requires an inner strength to go against the teachings of those who have been - and perhaps still are - important to you. In doing so, you risk rejection and denigration.

The young camper in my story had to overcome guilt and fear of rejection in order to declare her doubts. She required a well-developed ego to give her the courage and strength essential for breaking loose and making an authentic spiritual pilgrimage. Whenever people choose to hold onto established norms , *even when not fully believed,* or to abandon them in search of something truer, they are making a profound spiritual decision.

QUESTIONS FOR REFLECTION AND DISCUSSION

1. Who are your spiritual guides? With what persons do you surround yourself?

2. Has God ever failed to answer your prayers? Which ones? How did you handle it?

3. In what situations have you ever felt ignored or abandoned by God? What did you do?

4. How much freedom of the will do we have, really?

5. What have you abandoned in your pilgrimage?

6. What Sunday school teachings have you abandoned?

7. What doctrines or teachings of the church do you have difficulty in believing?

8. How has your God changed through the years?

9. How would you describe God today?

10. Where are you on your own personal pilgrimage:

     1. On schedule along a planned route?
     2. Roaming in the wilderness?
     3. Camping in an oasis?
     4. Safely arrived?
     5. Other? (e.g. Asleep at home. Hiding in a cave).

SCRIPTURAL REFERENCES

Exodus 3:14 God said to Moses, "I am who I am," And he said, "Say this to the people of Israel, 'I am has sent me to you.'"

Psalm 8: 3-4 When I look at the heavens, the works of thy fingers, the moon and the stars which thou hast established; what is man that thou art mindful of him, and the son of man that thou dost care for him?

Psalm 19: 1-4 The heavens are telling the glory of God; and the firmament proclaims His handiwork. Day to day pours forth speech, and night declares knowledge. There is no speech and there are no words; their voice is not heard; yet their voice goes out through all the earth, and their words to the end of the world.

Psalm 139:7-8 Whither shall I go from thy spirit? Or whither shall I flee from thy presence? If I ascend into heaven thou art there. If I descend into Sheol thou art there.

Job 40: 6-9 Then the Lord answered Job out of the whirlwind: "Gird up your loins like a man; I will question you and you will declare it to me. Will you put me in the wrong? Will you condemn me that you may be justified? Have you an arm like God, and can you thunder with a voice like His?"

Mark 14:36 And he said, "Abba, Father, all things are possible to thee; remove this Cup from me; yet not what I will, but what you wilt."

John 14:6-9 Jesus said to him, "I am the way, and the truth, and the life; no one comes to the Father but through me. If you had known me you would have known my Father also; henceforth you know him and have seen him." Philip said to him, "Lord, show us the Father, and we shall be satisfied." Jesus said to him, "Have I been with you so long, and yet you do not know me, Philip? He who has seen me has seen the Father. How can you say, 'Show us the Father?'"

John 14: 7 If you know me, you will know my Father also. From now on you do know him and have seen him."

Philippians 2:12 Not only in my presence, but more in my absence, work out your own salvation in fear and in trembling, for God is at work in you, both to will and to work for his good pleasure.

Ephesians 3:20 "Now unto him who is able to do immeasurably more than we can ask or imagine, by the power that is at work within us: to him be glory in the church and in Christ Jesus through all generations, forever and ever. Amen"

2. Can You Make the Buttons Even?

When I was a young boy living in the southeast corner of Detroit, morning was a rich experience. My mother was one of those persons who believed that breakfast was the most important meal of the day. By the time she called my brother and me for breakfast the kitchen was emitting marvelous odors, hinting of the feast to come. There would be fried grits or corn meal with bacon or ham or sausage. And there had to be eggs, scrambled, poached or fried over easy. Sometimes there were biscuits made from scratch. In winter, however, the morning ritual began with a tablespoon of cod liver oil, quickly washed down with a glass of orange juice which I swigged around to get the terrible feel and taste out of my mouth. After that I would tackle the better part of the breakfast. Whenever Granddad Cheatham visited I watched in fascination as he liberally sprinkled black pepper on his milk before every gulp. Whenever Grandmother Leslie was with us I could be certain she would engage me in some delightful banter bordering on debate, over whatever issue she thought might hook me.

As I said, morning was a rich experience. No matter how often or urgently Mom would remind us of the need for haste I usually headed for the door at the last moment, grabbing for whatever the weather called for on my way. In winter this usually required a bit more time. Michigan winters can be brutal. Coats, mittens, scarves, and headgear had to be in place prior to opening the door to receive the first blast of frigid air. I invariably began the buttoning process somewhere in the middle of my coat, donning hat and scarf between buttons. Often, in my haste, I began with the wrong button in the wrong hole. By the time I was finished part of the coat was scrunched up around my neck, while one side dangled limply alone at the bottom. In frustration I would turn to Mom and plaintively ask, "Can you make the buttons even?" In response she would begin unbuttoning them and then start the process from the bottom, saying, "Dick, if you get it right at the bottom it will come out right at the top."

When school was over I always rushed to go home with my older brother, George. As a five and six year old in a large school filled with bigger people, it seemed safer - more comfortable - to walk with George through the crowded halls and playground. In my rush to get ready I usually messed up the buttons again. When George came by my classroom he would gaze at me with that look one usually reserves for starving stray dogs. Then he would repeat the ritual and words of Mom, "Dick, if you get it right at the bottom it will come out right at the top."

Decades later I occasionally find myself rushing for the door while buttoning my shirt or coat on the way, only to end up with an uneven mess which chokes my throat and looks absurd. I stop and begin the process anew, as I long-ago had been taught. The words of Mom and brother George silently echo in my mind: "Dick, if you get it right at the bottom it will come out right at the top."

There are other times when it is not my clothing but my life, or my world, that does not seem to "fit" properly. Things are not going well, at work or within the family, or in some of the many other relationships which fill and enrich my life. I usually confront this by griping and blaming others or life's general circumstances for the misfit. When I finally settle down into reflective prayer, however, I often hear the voice of my older brother. It is not my brother George's voice, but my older brother and my Lord Jesus saying, "Dick, if you get it right at the bottom it will come out right at the top." *Seek first the Kingdom of God and its righteousness and all these things shall follow, as well. (Matthew 6:33).* Then in the silence of prayer God works with me to unbutton the errors of my life. God leads me back to the first misfit. It may be one I fastened incorrectly years ago. It may be one I just recently set wrong. Together we examine the problem and then begin to put things together so that the buttons of my life will be even. Then Romans 8:28

kicks in: *"For we know that in all things God works for the good with those who love Him and are called according to his purpose. "*

More often than not I realize that I have gotten the priorities of my life tangled. As a minister I may have become caught up in "the numbers game." This is quite easy to do. For the annual report we like to show that the church has grown under our leadership. We want to show more members, larger attendance, larger offerings. These are all signs of a strong and growing congregation. However, these should be the fruits, the side effects, of a successful ministry. They never should be the goal. When I allow them to slip into first place things invariably go badly. When we worry more about appearances than realities we've got the buttons out of order. We all know people with nice houses filled with gadgets. They walk about with smiling faces and the tailored look of success. Yet their lives are anything but abundant . . . or happy.

During more than forty years of ministry, countless individuals and couples have come into my office for a personal chat or visit. After the preliminaries, when they begin to open their souls, I hear them saying in various ways, "My life doesn't fit as it should. Can you make the buttons even?" At such moments I am tempted to repeat that oft-heard phrase from my childhood, "If you get it right at the bottom it will come out right at the top." I realize, however, that this would not make much sense to them. Then I'm tempted to cite Matthew 6:33, but usually dismiss that as not much better. These people think they believe in God. They believe they are seeking God's Kingdom. If I were to ask them, most would honestly say that they believe they really are attempting to do God's will in their lives. They believe they genuinely are seeking God's Kingdom. If they were to ask me to point the way, I could not play the part of the good witch and simply say, "Follow the yellow brick road." It's not that easy. Jesus himself said the road was narrow and few could stay on it. It's difficult to point the way in more than general terms. The path for each individual is personal and unique. We all begin in different places. Still, there are some general directions that should help to keep any of us on the proper path.

First, we Americans have difficulty in grasping the concepts inherent in the term, "Kingdom of God." The Gospel accounts do not say,

"Kingdom of God." The original Greek reads *Basileia tou Theou.* In the King James translation the term "Basileia" was translated as "kingdom." That is because England was a kingdom. If it had been ruled by an emperor, the better translation would have been, "empire." "Kingdom" is not the best translation for Americans. Try as I might, anytime I use that term my mind automatically conjures up some image akin to Disney's Magic Kingdom, complete with castle and walls. The people of England do not do this. They live in "The United Kingdom." They quite naturally envision what we envision when we use the term "nation." There are no castles, no walls, no moats, no narrow gates. The people of first century Judea understood what the term meant. They were being invited to become part of the nation of God, under the rule of God. Not Rome! Not Herod! There was no earthly ruler, guru or philosophy. This was a political as well as a spiritual statement. Only by becoming God's people would life begin to fall into place with genuine peace, prosperity, and plenitude.

Those of us who would "seek the Kingdom" have to learn what it actually means to live as the people of God. It is not just a matter of church attendance or the remembrance of a "saving moment" when Jesus became a genuine and vital part of our life. It must filter into the mainstream of our daily living as a deep-seated value which determines our choices and our actions.

The first century threat to the integrity of Judaism was Hellenism. The Grecian culture was rife with seductive beauty, low demands upon the individual, magical formulae, deities for every purpose, and social acceptance. Hellenism did not woo the faithful from Judaism. It infiltrated their synagogues and intermixed with their teachings. It distorted and diluted the demands of their faith. Today's comparative threat to Christianity is a combination of *modernity* and *materialism.* Each has blended into contemporary Christianity to produce the same results of dilution and distortion.

We shall look first at modernity. As I am using the term it is the continuation of the 17th - 18th century's Enlightenment. It may give lip service to God, but as a practical matter it constructs life as though God were irrelevant. Modernity places its trust in science, technology, and social standing. Personal pleasure takes priority over any sense of responsibility to God. When confronted with a choice between the personal (or children's) sports, cultural, social responsibilities, and church participation, the choice inevitably favors the former. "It is important that our children have this opportunity," is the standard explanation. Church attendance is not considered as *required*. Rather it is *optional*. Participation in secular events takes precedence over religious offerings or duties. Religious life is, at best, compartmentalized. What is preached on a Sunday is not integrated into the listener's professional, social, or family life. We all have participated to some degree in modernity. It is rampant! Our money may proclaim "In God We Trust," but our lives suggest otherwise.

Materialism is not synonymous with "greed." Simply stated it is the belief that material things make life good and worthy. To be sure, material things can enhance the quality of life in many ways. I believe we all can agree to that. Materialism, however, puts primary emphasis on *things*. Marx's Communism, for example, believed in materialistic determinism. Marx professed (and the people believed) that the proper amount of material goods, properly distributed, would cancel all economic exploitation and political strife, and create a utopian society. We in America tend to share that belief on a more personalized basis. A nicer house will create a better home for *our* family A better school building will create a better education for *our* children We believe that if we have enough money and enough things *our* lives will be safe, serene, joyful, and good. As a consequence we work ourselves to death in order to earn more money and purchase more things. We now claim to have the highest standard of living in human history. Yet, half of our marriages fail. Spousal and child abuse are epidemic. Violence is widespread. Too many high school graduates are functionally illiterate. Credit card default and personal bankruptcy are epidemic. Our rich get richer and our poor become disproportionately poorer. "Downsizing," which translates into firing employees in order to bolster corporation profits, is standard practice as management abandons loyalty to the workers who made them wealthy. Labor, on the other hand, appears to feel little loyalty to management. Employee theft and absenteeism are more than minor problems. Our prisons are overflowing, and we have turned the mentally ill into the streets in order to save ourselves tax dollars.

Examine the way you spend your money and your time if you want to make your buttons even. Show me your checkbook and your personal calendar and you will have shown me much of your value system. These are the bottom buttons of your life. If they are not in the proper place, nothing else will fit correctly. Take a look at them. Are you comfortable with them? Do they represent what you want your life to be - what you want your soul to become?

People are for loving and things are for using. When you find yourself loving things and using people you are in trouble.

If you are buttoning your life in the middle it is no wonder that your life does not fit as it should. So how do we make the buttons of our society even? It will not be through government intervention. Governments are neither designed nor equipped to reform society. They are at best a reflection of the values and mores of the people they govern. It will not be through the manufacturing or banking establishments. Their tasks are simply to produce goods and/or to generate profits. Nor will it be through the school system. Parents err in putting the tasks of child-rearing and moral instruction in that arena. It is all the schools can do to teach many of the undisciplined and overly-indulged children who are foisted off on them. Whenever we look to others for relief or reform we are casting ourselves as victims. "Save us! Save us! " is the cry of those who cannot - or will not - save themselves. It is not the cry of those who would be genuinely free.

I can offer but one suggestion: *If you get it right at the bottom it will come out right at the top.* You probably will not change the whole of society. You may only begin to transform your life and the lives of some of those akin to you. It might not be all you want but it is the advice and the challenge which Jesus places before you. The second part of his challenge is as important as the first: " . . . and its righteousness." To be among God's people means to attempt to do God's will. The Greek term which we translate as "righteousness" is *dikaiosune*. It denotes a righteousness that is greater than the "We don't smoke and we don't chew and we don't go with girls who do," variety which stops just short of being "goody goody two shoes." It calls for more than just not doing something that is considered bad. It calls for setting right those things that are wrong. This is true both for your personal life and the existing social situations. There are many inequities in life. We tend to ignore them or to dismiss them as inevitable. Family chores and priorities may be out of kilter, or at least seem that way to some. Certainly our society has many injustices which may seem small to us but loom large to those who suffer from them. God's righteousness calls for becoming part of the solution and not just complaining or waiting for someone else to make the buttons fit.

I moved to San Antonio in 1998. It is a beautiful city with winters far more pleasant than those in which I was raised. They have a professional basketball team named "The Spurs." When I arrived the Spurs had not won a championship in their twenty- six year history. Since I was a life-long Detroit Lion fan I felt right at home. Our hope would always be in "next year." Yet there was something special about this Spurs team. The players did not seem at all like the egocentric, greedy, amoral crew I had grown to expect from professional basketball players. Their long-time star, David Robinson, is an outstanding example of class and sportsmanship. A newer -star-in-the-making, Tim Duncan, had arrived on the scene. When asked, David agreed to step back and play a lesser role in the offense in order to provide a stronger defense. This meant that there would be fewer headlines proclaiming David as the scoring star of the game, "The Man" who got the ball when the chips were down. It would also mean less bargaining power at salary negotiation time. I listened to David's language and quickly picked up that he is a person of deep religious convictions. I had to learn more about him. He and his wife have donated five million dollars to a prep school and cultural center to be constructed in one of the needier sections of San Antonio. David also promised a class of fifth graders that when they graduated from high school he would give each graduate two thousand dollars to help with their education. It was obvious that David Robinson believed it was wrong for young people to be deprived of an education in this wealthy land of ours. He therefore began to set things right, at least in his area of influence. He has also instituted and supervises a "Feed

My Sheep" program. Again, because he believes it is wrong for people to starve in a land of abundance. That is another wrong which calls to be set right. When asked about his sacrifice his response was, "If I'm busy clutching my money with both hands, how am I going to be able to hug my wife and children?"

It was nice to see David and the Spurs win the NBA title that year. When asked about the celebration David told the reporters that they were asking the wrong person. He said he had gone back to his hotel room with his son because he had promised his son he could sleep with him if they won the championship. When I heard that I knew that David did not profess one belief and practice another. This man was actively trying to be one of God's people, doing what he could to make life better - fairer - for others. In the process, life was working well for him. When asked to kiss the trophy, he laughingly responded, "I don't kiss anything that doesn't kiss me back." He said the hardware (trophy and rings) were nice, but what he and his teammates would prize and remember was what they had accomplished as a team. They had built trust and teamwork. Everyone had done what was necessary for the good of the entire team. I thought it quite fitting that the "Good Guys" finished first, and David finally removed the stigma of not being able to "win it all." Even if they had fallen short in the playoffs, however, David and the other Spurs could not have been labeled "Losers." These people were "Winners" in the purest sense of the word. /

This is the kind of activity Jesus was calling for with his phrase, ". . . and its righteousness." The rest then falls in place quite naturally, ". . . and all these things shall be yours as well." Imagine, if you will, a workplace where every person does what needs to be done for the good of the entire group; a family in which every person does the same; a community in which all members pitch in and work for the well-being of every other member. This is not going to happen in our lifetime. However, for those few who do begin working for the Kingdom, life will become better. Their lives will fit more comfortably. They will live less like victims and more like victors. A fellowship of the faithful will emerge, and they will live more of their lives within that community. Essentially they will have become part of the People of God, seeking to set things right in their world. They will have *entered* into the Kingdom.

So how do you go about making the buttons of your life even? Stop looking to other people - either as saviors or as scapegoats. Instead, look to your own life. This will require unusual honesty in examining your values and priorities. As I said earlier, "Show me your checkbook and your personal calendar and you will have shown me much of your value system." Listen to some of the words of Jesus on the subject:

Where your treasure is there will be your heart, also. (Matthew 6:21)

Not everyone who calls me, "Lord, Lord" will enter the Kingdom of Heaven, but only those who do the will of my Father in Heaven. (Matthew 7:21)

Begin carefully unbuttoning those buttons that do not belong where they are. Grab the proper bottom button firmly, and start over anew. If you get it right at the bottom it *will* come out right at the top.

Seek first the Kingdom of God and its righteousness, and all these things shall be yours as well. (Matthew 6:33)

1 The Spurs won the NBA Championship again in 2003, and David Robinson retired on top.

REFLECTIONS

There are no shortcuts. There are no guaranteed formulas for success in *any* venture. However, one cannot ignore the basics and hope to succeed. We have a constant inner dialogue which calls us in differing directions. Those who superimpose the world view of the first century into our present culture, or who merely find it more comfortable to project the shadow part of our personality onto outside forces, might claim they were being tempted by Satan. Be that as it may, the voices and the dialogue continue. The journey to wholeness necessarily involves dialogue and struggle between our inner opposing forces. It is within this inner turmoil that harmony and wholeness will eventually emerge.

Those who would be intentional about the paths their souls will take would do well to reinforce those voices which sound more noble - more worthy. In our better moments we might try to put on the full armor of God, as Paul suggested in Ephesians 6:13-18. The inner work of prayer and reflection are good starting points. It is not enough, however, to think good thoughts, and to verbalize caring concern for others and for injustices. The intentional pilgrim would do well to heed the words of James 1:22: *"Be doers of the word and not hearers only, deceiving yourselves."* It is in actualizing our faith in the arena of life that those qualities become genuine and vital. The buttons are both mental and physical.

QUESTIONS FOR REFLECTION AND DISCUSSION

1. Have you seen others whose world did not fit because their buttons were out of order?.

2. When, if ever, have you felt *your* world was not fitting as it should, only to discover that your priorities were out of order?

3. What were you able to do about it?

4. How does one go about seeking the Kingdom in today's world?

5. Who are some of the people you know who actively are seeking the Kingdom?

6. Has societal pressure ever restrained you from pursuing righteousness? How?

7. In what ways have modernity and materialism altered society's faith during your lifetime?

8. In what ways have modernity and materialism affected *your* faith?

SCRIPTURAL REFERENCES

Matthew 6:21 "For where your treasure is, there your heart will be also."

Matthew 6: 33 "But seek first His Kingdom and His righteousness, and all these things will be given to you as well."

Matthew 7:21 "Not everyone who says to me, 'Lord, Lord,' but only the one who does the will of my heavenly Father."

Romans 8:28 "For we know that in all things God works for the good with those who love Him and are called according to His purpose."

Ephesians 6:13-18 "Therefore take the whole armor of God, that will be able to withstand in the evil day and having done all, to stand. Stand therefore having girded your loins with truth, and having put on the breastplate of righteousness, and having shod your feet with the equipment of the gospel of peace. Besides all this, having taken the shield of faith, with which you can quench all the flaming darts of the evil one. And take the helmet of salvation and the sword of the spirit, which is the word of God. Pray at all times in the Spirit with all prayer and supplication. To that end keep alert with all perseverance, making supplication for all the saints."

3. ECHOES FROM THE PAST

I was serving my first congregation, a student charge in Napoleon, Michigan. It was a quiet, Saturday morning, and I planned to spend some of the little free time I had with my young family. However, the telephone rang. It was one of the young girls from the congregation calling for me. She was a fragile, lovely, young lady of about eighteen years of age. Her voice was urgent - almost desperate: "Rev. Cheatham," she said, "I need your help." She quickly explained that her father had shoved his automatic 45 caliber service pistol into her stomach and told her, "I probably ought to shoot the both of us and just end it." Then he had gone into the kitchen and was sitting there as we spoke, trying to decide what he should do.

I gave my wife, Diane, a special hug and headed for the girl's house. I had never met her father. She was new to the congregation. I barely knew her. I had no idea what sort of man I was about to meet. From her words I assumed there was no mother in the house. I arrived and found the father, still in the kitchen, sitting at the table, gun in hand . . . staring blankly at the wall. I pulled up a chair and sat down across from him, thinking to myself that seminary had never prepared me for anything like this. He looked at me, silently sizing me up. Then he placed his pistol on the table, and slowly began to tell me his story. He had been a master sergeant in an intelligence unit in the Pacific Theater of Operations during World War II. It had been his task to select two members of his unit to accompany the first wave of troops to hit the beach in every invasion landing.

The two men always were slain.

He repeatedly attempted to give this task back to his unit commander. However, the commander wanted the task no more than he did and simply declined. So before every landing he had to select two men he *knew* would be killed. He knew they would die, and he knew them personally as friends. Still he assigned them. They went. They died. He managed to return from the war without any physical wounds. The damage to his soul, however, was enormous. He continually heard echoes from the past which told him he should not be alive, that he did not deserve to be alive, and that he was unworthy of anyone's love.

I tried to draw upon his faith, but there was none available. Still, he calmed a bit as we talked. Finally he arose and put his pistol back in the drawer. I sensed the crisis was past. I left the kitchen, gave a word of assurance to his daughter, and returned home.

On the return home I reflected upon what had transpired. I surmised that his daughter also had her echoes from the past. Certainly her parents had imparted their damaged spirits which had weakened her potential and limited her opportunities. There are occasions when the sins and brokenness of the parents actually are visited to their children. I resolved to become better acquainted with her. She, at least, was in the church and open to God's healing grace. I learned that her father had been married and divorced five times. Her mother (his first wife) obviously had her own echoes and weakening spirits. She, too, had been married and divorced numerous times. This lovely young girl (let's call her Laura) had bounced back and forth between her parents, depending upon whose marriage was most stable at the time. Her echoes told her that no relationship lasts. When they would go bad, as invariably they would, she should flee for safety.

Some time later she met a fine young man who understood her and genuinely cared for her. In due course they fell in love and decided to marry. In our premarital counseling sessions I cautioned her about her echoes and infirming spirits. She dismissed my concerns, saying she never could leave this young man who loved her so dearly. However, when their relationship slipped off the mountain top into a valley (all relationships have peaks and valleys) she fled. Eventually she returned, a bit wiser about the power of her echoes. This time she began working upon erasing them and replacing them with affirming messages.

Echoes from the past can produce spirits of infirmity which limit our lives and cause us to become far less than God would have us be. Sometimes these echoes are so subtle that we are unaware of their shaping effect.

A minister colleague spoke of a Canadian clergyman who stood before his congregation one Sunday and made a startling confession. He said that for thirty-five years he had believed he was worshiping and serving Jesus Christ. Now he realized he had been worshiping something quite different. It could be summed up in these two words: "Measure up!" He confessed that most of what he had accomplished through his years of ministry had not been for the benefit of the Kingdom or in obedience to Jesus Christ. Rather they were the results of an unconscious attempt to *measure up* to the standards set by others, or arbitrarily imposed by himself. When I heard his story I thought of my own annual conference of clergy. The statistician's report is the most carefully studied document in the entire conference manual. So many feel the need to see how they measure up with their peers. Is their church as large or larger? Is their attendance as good or better? Is their salary as high or higher? They measure their self-worth, their success as pastors by how they *measure up* to others.

I would venture that somewhere along life's pathway they had received various admonitions *to measure up*: in the classroom, in athletics, in social status, and practically any other activity you can name. I would also venture that it is not only clergy who suffer from this malady, that it is more or less universal. We constantly read of some athlete who is paid millions of dollars per year, who threatens to sit out the season if he is not paid as much - or more - than some rival athlete. So many of our own decisions concerning profession, expenditures, housing, clothing, and general life styles factor in the need to *measure up*. We want our possessions to reflect an image of success and worthiness. I sometimes believe our highways become just one more arena for people to surpass their peers.

The irony of all this is that all our craving to measure up may, indeed, drive us to succeed professionally and economically. However, it never allows us to lean back and enjoy the fruits of our labors. We must measure up tomorrow, and the tomorrow after that. We cannot stop the race the moment we are out in front.

Once I opened the Pandora's box of past echoes, an endless number began to pour forth. Let me mention a few:

On Sunday mornings, when I look at the congregation while they are singing a hymn I always see a few whose lips are not moving. Some bear pained expressions as they either stand silently or mumble their way through the verses. These pained expressions and unmoving lips belong to people whose echoes tell them they cannot sing. Perhaps with some men it is an echo which tells them that singing is for sissies. Years earlier when they first began to sing someone told them that they could not, or should not, and they believed them. As a consequence they can never enter entirely into the full joy of worship. For them hymn singing will always be a painful activity. Now I rather imagine that when these same people first began to walk or to talk they did not do that very well either. However, no one told them that they could not walk or talk. Instead they probably were given words of encouragement. As a consequence, today they can walk and talk acceptably. Still, I know far too many people whose self-identification is that they cannot carry a tune in a basket.

There are many intelligent people who cannot sing - cannot draw - cannot dance - cannot do something which most normal people are capable of learning to do acceptably - simply because someone's negative comments have placed a spirit of infirmity within their souls.

I relate to this issue quite personally in a couple of ways. I have a daughter who thoroughly enjoyed singing when she was little. Her ear was not fine-tuned yet, and occasionally she sang in the cracks. Still, she had a pleasant voice and found much enjoyment in singing as best she could. A lot of children sing a bit "uncertainly" in their early years. Most of them eventually learn to sing "close enough." However, my daughter had the great misfortune of having a singing teacher publicly chide her for not being able to sing on pitch. Today she no longer sings. I realize now that when I was a child I sang in the cracks a great deal of the time. The difference is that no one told me that my singing was bad. My mother had the habit of singing as she did her daily household chores, and she let me sing along whenever I felt like chiming in. She never spoke a word of criticism, although she must have been silently praying that my ear would improve. Years later, I understand why the junior choir director would greet me with tears in her eyes. Still, she never criticized me. She let me make a joyful noise unto the Lord, allowing me to refine my pitch according to my own time schedule. Without an infirming spirit to hinder me I eventually learned to sing, and even sang the lead in my college musical. It has added a wonderful dimension to my life, and I shall forever be grateful to those "silent saints" who allowed me to sing.

On the other hand I did receive a spirit of infirmity while growing up. As a child I was determined to learn to play the clarinet. I practiced hours every day and studied under one of the finest clarinet teachers in the country. When I was in the ninth grade I was first chair solo in my high school band. The next year I was selected to be first chair solo in the all-state band. I should have known that I played reasonably well. However, my instructor probably felt that I needed to be constantly prodded to keep me from becoming self-satisfied and complacent. This is the message that he constantly gave to me at my lessons (he was Italian so I will express it as it came to me):

"Dick-a-my-boy, you one-a-nice-a-fella, but you no-can-play the clarinet."

For years, performing was painful for me. I am not referring to the nervousness which most people experience prior to performing. The entire experience from beginning to afterglow was painful. Throughout the performance I believed the audience was enduring it rather than enjoying it. Afterward, no matter how others might compliment me I dismissed them thinking, "If you really knew the clarinet you would know that I was not very good." The negative words of one person who really mattered drowned out all the positive words that came my way.

It took many years to get that out of my system. First I had to erase the old message. Actually this can never be completely accomplished. You will always hear the dim echoes. Still, I did this in part by reinterpreting the negative words, by trying to understand the reason for them. Next, I began to cover over the tape with the many positive messages I had received, accepting them instead of discounting them. Finally I was able to silence that old negative echo and actually enjoy producing the music I had worked so hard to create.

One day I came across this passage from II Timothy 1:7 *"For God did not give you a spirit of timidity, but rather a spirit of power, and of love, and of self-discipline."* This helped explain what I had understood intuitively. Fear, perhaps, is the basis for our infirming spirits. Any kind of fear will do, *e.g.* fear of failure, of criticism, of pain. Self-doubt generates fear. Laura's tendency to flee from difficult situations was caused by her fear. The need to measure up produces a form of fear. The common echo, "What will other people think?" elicits another form of fear. This, incidentally, has magnificent potential for strapping the soul and killing all creativity. If we succumb to this fear, God's will for our lives will never take precedence over the need to win the approval of others. The more insecure we feel about ourselves the greater will be our need to prove our worth to others.

I have learned that a great source of affirmation is to be found in Scripture. I am convinced that their writers were inspired. I further believe that when you read Scripture faithfully you can discern the Word of God addressing you through their words. These are the words which have the power to override the destructive echoes of the past which have given you your spirits of infirmity.

The touchstone Scripture of my life has become Romans 8:28: *"For we know that in all things God works for the good with those who love Him and are called according to His purpose."* All situations have a way of deteriorating. Things can go bad. Like most of you I have received enough negative messages to justify wallowing in self- recrimination, or self-pity - and blaming others, or just waiting to be rescued by those stronger and more competent than I. However, this message can override all those negative echoes with the spirit of power and love and self-discipline of which of which II Timothy speaks. I have learned to blend the passage from Romans with Matthew 7:7, however: *"Ask and you shall receive, seek and you shall find, knock and it will be opened to you."* I have come to recognize that God does not always give what is asked for. Rather He gives what is needed at that moment. Your asking opens you to receive what is being offered. Similarly, I rarely find what it is I am seeking, but once again, if I am open to see what *is* available I can find what it is God wants to me have at that particular moment. Have you ever knocked on someone's door (or rang their doorbell) and no one appeared to be home, then you hear someone calling from the back yard or side door? That is how my knocking generally works. The door I am pounding on may remain closed, but another . . . somewhere . . . opens for me. If I am paying attention to what God may be doing I will notice that door and go where God wishes to lead me. Understanding these things has changed my life. I no longer believe there are dead ends . . . even when we take our final earthly breath.

I recall a survey that was made back in the 1960's. People residing in retirement and nursing homes were questioned about their attitudes toward death. Surprisingly, elderly Christians were more afraid of dying than non-Christians. They were fearful of the approaching Judgment, whereas non-Christians had no belief in such a judgment. It is tragic that the Good News of Jesus Christ should generate fear in some of his believers. In far too many instances the Good News has become distorted into *bad* news by broken people living in a broken society. They are guided more by their own spirits of infirmity than by the Spirit of the Living God. They may be well-intentioned, but they are misguided. I must tell you that the prevailing definition of sin as a kind of spiritual virus which permeates the soul is not to be found in the teachings of Jesus. The primary biblical word we translate as "sin" (*harmatano*) literally means to "fall short," to "miss the mark," or to "fail." When we read of Jesus telling a person, "Your sins are forgiven," we would do well to translate that as "Your failures (moral, ethical, social, etc.) are forgiven." As fallible human beings we fall short and miss the mark with regularity. We all share Paul's dilemma *"For I do not do the good I want but the evil I do not want is what I do."* Romans 7:19) It appears we have been made this way: Failing to accomplish

31

our highest goals, straying from our chosen paths, committing mental errors. Jesus words were simple and straightforward: "Your failings (*harmatano*) are forgiven." (Mark 2:5) He knew we were burdened by our failures, and he lifted those burdens. Part of the Good News is that these human failings should not be a burden which weighs heavily on our souls, diminishing the joys of living, and making us fearful of God. Paul says this clearly in his letter to the Corinthians (II Cor. 5:17-19): *"If anyone is in Christ that person is a new creation. The old has passed away and the new has come. All this is from God who was in Christ reconciling the world to himself, not counting our sins against us, but entrusting us with the message of salvation."*

Paul himself had been transformed from an angry bigot, full of himself, into an apostle who was capable of writing the beautiful love passage found in I Corinthians 13. This metamorphosis occurred within Paul when he turned from the messages of the world and embraced Jesus Christ.

If you ever are fully to receive God's spirit of freedom and empowerment you finally must turn off those disabling echoes of the past, and stop carrying around those burdens caused by past mistakes and misdeeds. If possible, you must try to make things right with those who may have been injured. That is quite different from toting around the guilt and shame. Take the echoes to God in prayer. Offer them to Him. Leave them there. For some this will prove easy. For others it may seem nearly impossible. We have received those messages which say, "Do not reveal your weaknesses," or "you can do it on your own." This is one reason so many men refuse to go to a counselor, ("I can ruin my marriage or go crazy without anyone's help."). I have observed far too many people toting their heavy burdens who simply cannot let them go. Some are obviously weighed down. Others mask it well, but still bear that weight within themselves. Many is the time that I have silently sung the words from that old hymn, "Oh what peace we often forfeit. Oh what needless pain we bear, all because we do not carry everything to God in prayer." Jesus said," *Come unto me you who are weary and are heavily burdened, and I will give you rest. Take my yoke upon you and learn from me; for I am gentle and lowly in heart, and you will find rest for your souls. For my yoke is easy and my burden is light.* (Matthew 11: 28-30) Let those unnecessary burdens go and allow the spirit of power, or love, and of self-discipline to enter into your life.

In my first church a young high school senior, Alex, approached me one evening and asked me if I really believed what I had preached that morning. It had been a sermon expounding the possibilities God gives us in life. I assured Alex that if I preached it I believed it. I realized that he was asking a more personal, more profound question, so I waited for it to follow. I was aware that Alex' older brother was academically gifted. Alex was bright but he could not compete with his brother in the classroom. On the other hand Alex was a fine athlete and his brother was not able to compete in *that* arena, so Alex had staked his claim there and had left the classroom to his brother. Alex explained to me that some while back his counselor had told him that he was not college material. He had accepted that diagnosis and had resigned himself to his lot in life. My sermon, as he had personalized it, had suggested to him that he might be able to succeed in college if he had the commitment to do the work. I paraphrased Philippians 4:13 to him: *"[You] can do all things through the one who empowers you."* Then I added, "But you will have to work as hard on your studies as you do on your jump shot." Alex appeared to believe me and you could see his spirits lift immediately. The spirit of infirmity given him by a thoughtless counselor was replaced by the empowering spirit of God the moment he could believe the Good News as it applied to his daily life. That final semester he managed to make the academic honor roll for the first time in his life. He went on to graduate from a local Methodist College (where he also lettered in basketball). That was the last I heard of Alex. Many years later his name came up in a conversation my wife, Diane, and I were having. A young lady in the congregation heard his name and excitedly jumped into our conversation. Alex had been her high school principal. She went on to say that he was a much-loved and highly respected principal. I would venture a guess that he never placed a spirit of infirmity on any of his students. Rather, he would have worked to empower them as he himself had been empowered. What Alex had discovered was the truth of Paul's statement that *"anyone who is in Christ is a new Creation. The old has passed away and the new has* come." *(II Corinthians 5:17)* He had experienced the reality of Paul's word, *"I can do all things through the one who empowers me."* 1

1 The popular translation reads, *"I can do all things through Christ who strengthens me."* However, the Greek does not say "Christ." It says *"outos"* which translates as "the one." Also the Greek *"dunamos"* best translates as "empowers," which I find to be a far more powerful term than "strengthens."

REFLECTIONS

None of us makes it to adulthood without having suffered wounds of the spirit. The childhood slogan, "Sticks and stones may break my bones, but words will never hurt me." are words of bravado used to cover the hurt that has been inflicted. With time, we find that most physical wounds heal, while the spiritual wounds inflicted by cruel or thoughtless words continue to fester in our souls. I still have vivid memories of the moments when some of those words were thrust into my soul. I would venture that many readers do, as well. Somewhere within almost every person I know there is a wounded, frightened little child, who does not really believe he or she is capable of achieving the desired goals of life. One task of adulthood - a task essential for spiritual maturity or wholeness - is to heal those wounds. They disable us in ways we do not realize, causing us to withhold ourselves, or our gifts, from others. They keep us in the shadows of life rather than allowing us to venture forth into the more public arenas. They burden us with feelings of inadequacy. If we attempt to deny or merely bury those feelings, they burrow further into our unconscious and become part of our shadow personality. Then we may project those "inadequacies" onto others in some vain attempt to elevate ourselves above them. The words of Jesus in Matthew 7:1-3 relate to this:

Judge not, that you not be judged, for with the judgment you pronounce you will be judged, and the measure you give will be the measure you get. Why do you see the speck in your brother's eye but do not notice the log that is in your eye?

In short, Jesus is saying that you probably tell more about yourself when you criticize others, than you do about them. Our old, untended wounds create more havoc than we realize.

We also have inherited patterns of actions and reactions. As the young lady was preconditioned to flee from difficult relationships, so we have pre-programmed ways of responding to various stimuli in our lives. As long as we remain unconscious of these, they control our reactions and we will repeat them. The only way to become free is to recognize them for what they are, and make a conscious choice to change. It is amazing how the mere recognition of these controlling patterns can free us of their power. I believe these are at least some of the inner demons which Jesus exorcised by naming and dismissing. It also gives a new way of understanding his words, *"If you continue in my word, then you are my disciples indeed, and you shall know the truth and the truth will set you free."* (John 8:31-32) To continue in Jesus' word is to remain consciously aware of the quest for authenticity. We will look inward - not outward - for the demons, for the cause of our problems. Rather than rationalize our actions we will examine them, and in that process we will name them , cast them out, and be free.

QUESTIONS FOR REFLECTION AND DISCUSSION

1. What echoes from the past have given you a spirit of infirmity?

2. What can you do to quiet those echoes?

3. How do echoes contribute to whatever prejudices you have?

4. How do they contribute to prejudices in general?

5. Do you know someone who carries spirits of infirmity because of past echoes?

6. What Bible passages could you share to override those negative messages?

SCRIPTURAL REFERENCES

Matthew 7:1-3   Judge not, that you not be judged, for with the judgment you pronounce you will be judged, and the measure you give will be the measure you get. Why do you see the speck in your brother's eye but do not notice the log that is in your eye?

Matthew 7:7   Ask and it will be given you; seek and you will find; knock and it will be opened to you.

Matthew 11:28-30 Come unto me you who are weary and are heavily burdened, and I will give you rest. Take my yoke upon you and learn from me; for I am gentle and lowly in heart, and you will find rest for your souls. For my yoke is easy and my burden is light.

Mark 2:5   And when Jesus saw their faith he said to the paralytic, "My son, your sins are forgiven."

Romans 8:28   For we know that all things work for the good with those who love God and are called according to his purpose.

II Corinthians 5:17-19   Therefore if anyone is in Christ he is a new creation; the old has passed away, behold, the new has come. All this is from God who through Christ reconciled us to himself and gave us the ministry of reconciliation; that is God was in Christ reconciling the world to himself not counting their trespasses against them, and entrusting to us the message of reconciliation.

Philippians 4:13   I can do all things through the one who empowers me.

II Timothy 1:7   God did not give you a spirit of timidity, but a spirit of power and love and self-control.

4. LET IT GO

It was the last day of my first year at Wentworth Military Academy in Lexington, Missouri. I went into the bathroom to clean up and prepare for our final parade and dismissal ceremony. I arrived at the sink at about the same time as another cadet. We were not close companions but if either of us had been asked we probably would have described ourselves as "friends." We jostled one another, each claiming rights to the sink. I thought we were being playful. Then, unexpectedly, the other cadet's eyes flashed fire. He put up his fists and challenged me to a fight. In this era, when you were challenged, you were honorbound to accept. It was the manly thing to do. Whether you won or lost was not so important as your display of courage. For some reason, not clear to me at that moment, I simply did not want to fight him. I said something to the effect of, "Take it. It's yours." Then I turned and walked away. My roommate, who had been a Golden Glove Boxing finalist that year, asked me why I had not fought him. "You could have beaten him," he exclaimed. I shook my head silently. I had no answer. It was not fear. It was something quite different, which I had never experienced.

After the formal dismissal I walked back to the barracks. It was time to pack my belongings and return home for the summer. As I walked I saw this friend from the morning's encounter. He smiled at me, ran across the street, and began to shake my hand fervently (men did not hug in those days). We wished one another well for the summer - then farewell, for he had graduated and would not return. We parted as friends. As I continued my walk toward the barracks I felt a deep sense of satisfaction that our final remembrance of one another would be this moment, and not one of anger and violence.

I did not realize it at the time but I had taken a first step toward Christian maturity. The apostle Paul wrote, *"When I was a child, I spoke as a child, I thought as a child, I reasoned as a child. When I became a man I put away childish things."* (I Corinthians 13:11) Fighting would have been childish. It never was - never could be - the *manly* thing to do. I have never used my fists in anger since that day.

At this point I believe I should cite Philippians 3:12: *"Do not think I have accomplished all of this, or that I have already reached perfection, but I press on to take hold of that for which Christ has taken hold of me."* Remember, I said this was my *first* step, not my *final* step.

My next step began two years later and was attained about ten years after that time. Again, it was at Wentworth Military Academy. By this time I was a cadet captain, commander of Headquarters Company. I was the ranking officer in my barracks. Football practice had just ended. My roommate and I were sitting in our chairs, covered only by wrap-around towels. Football equipment was strewn about on the floor. Without a knock, our room door was opened. Someone stepped in and stood quietly. Since I was ranking officer I assumed this unknown visitor was standing at attention, waiting for me to give permission for him to move or speak. I let him stand for a few seconds (good for his discipline . . . and my ego). When I turned to see who it was I saw a faculty officer whom I did not recognize surveying the room with a look of disgust. "Oops," I thought. "It's time for *me* to be standing at attention." As I stood, I dimly recalled some scuttlebutt about a new assistant to the commandant being hired. This officer, a young man in his twenties, looked at me and exclaimed, "If this is the way in which you organize your life you would not last as a captain in the army for ten minutes."

Not having read Carnegie's book on *How to Win Friends and Influence People* I responded, "If this is the kind of guff I would have to take I would not want to last as a captain in the army for ten minutes." Although it was emotionally satisfying for me at the time it was not a wise response for me to give. It initiated a feud that was to last for the entire academic year. Whenever he was the inspector for the barracks I could expect a room demerit. I soon learned that he had not been an officer in the army. I also learned that while he had been a cadet at the academy he had never been an officer. Naturally, I used this information to give him little reminders that I was, in fact, superior to him.

Needless to say we did not rush to embrace one another at the end of that year.

A few years passed. The Korean War broke out. I accepted a commission and went on active duty. I even attained the rank of captain. Normally I never would have written the school to tell them of my accomplishments. However, in this instance I somehow felt compelled to inform them of this promotion . Sometime later I returned to the academy for a homecoming event. After a couple of days I realized I had not seen my old nemesis. Under the circumstances I thought it might be nice to see him for a moment (to resume our game of one-upmanship, I assume). When I inquired about him the response was, "That was really tragic." He had acquired Lou Gerhig's Disease. His wife had abandoned him. He had died alone in severe pain.

. . . I never felt so petty in all my life.

I had been privately nurturing a grudge and feelings of superiority toward him. I should have been praying for him instead. In a moment of clarity I realized that he actually was a decent person, just as I was a decent person. We simply had let our egos get in the way. We each had refused to see our contribution in the breakdown between us. In order to justify ourselves we had mentally demonized the other person, and made ourselves the hero in the conflict.

I had much to learn about what Jesus meant in telling us to turn the other cheek in Matthew 5:38-39. He had prefaced that statement with *"Do not think that I have come to abolish the law or the prophets. I have not come to abolish but to fulfill."* When Moses gave the Law to the children of Israel they were a motley collection of tribes. They were not yet a cohesive nation. Their primary loyalty was to their tribe. If, for example, someone from the tribe of Dan injured someone from the tribe of Judah it would set off a blood feud between the tribes. Each would attempt to exact revenge from the other. There were no rules

- no laws - for ending such a feud. Moses proclaimed a law which said that the injured party could exact the same injury upon the guilty party: an eye for an eye; a tooth for a tooth. Quid pro quo. Then it was to be considered even - done - ended! The purpose never was to exact revenge. Rather, it was to put a stop to the violence as quickly as possible, with as little damage as seemed necessary.

When our children are young and immature, if one was to break the toy of another we might say, "Then you must give one of your toys to the person whose toy you broke, and that will make it even." No more bickering. No more fighting. By the time our children have matured into their teens, however, I hope we would merely say, "Forget it. It was an accident. These things happen in a family. Let it go." In a similar manner Jesus was merely upgrading the purpose of the law to what he believed was their level of maturity.

Paul understood this principle and amplified upon it in his letter to the Romans (12:17). *"Do not repay evil for evil. Try always to do what is right in the eyes of everyone."* In 12:21 he adds, *"Do not overcome evil with evil, but overcome evil with good."* He then takes the idea even further in his letter to the Ephesians (4:26), saying, *"In your anger do not sin. Do not let the sun set on your anger, and do not give the devil a foothold."* Paul understood that nourished anger festers in the soul to become hatred and bitterness. It degrades us, causing us to become far less than God would have us be. It does no earthly good.

I have come to understand that it is our egocentricity which causes us to become easily angered, and to nurture that anger into hatred. When I read the scriptural accounts of Jesus becoming angry, as in his clearing the Temple, I realize it is never egocentric anger. Rather, his anger is one of righteous outrage. There is an injustice - a violation of God's Will - which must be set right. He harnesses the energy from the anger and acts to set things right. He carries no grudges. Jesus never is self-centered. He always is God-centered.

The tactical officer from the academy and I let the sun set on our anger. We nourished it. We fed on it. We generated a feud from it. We were so focused on ourselves that we could never understand the

40

other person as anything but a problem. I have seen this phenomenon destroy marriages, divide families, ruin friendships, and create chaos in the workplace. Individuals and groups choose to pit themselves against one another rather than attempting to create understanding that would generate harmony and teamwork.

In the early days of my ministry a couple who had been feuding for most of their married lives came to me for counseling. There was absolutely no progress so we agreed to give up on the effort. They separated and the marriage appeared to be at its end. Then some time later, on the eve of their twenty-fifth wedding anniversary, they agreed to meet me in a neutral setting for one last try. I felt heartened and agreed. At the appointed time I arrived at the site, entered the house, and saw the couple. They were sitting in an unlighted room, staring at each other from opposite walls. As the time passed the room grew increasingly darker, not just from the lack of physical light, but from the oppressive emotional atmosphere. Try as I might I could not get them to stay on the subject of seeking common ground. Instead, each recited a lengthy litany of wrongs suffered at the hands of the other. Each accusation was met with an angry rebuttal. Finally I called out: "Stop! If you have any decency, get a divorce and stop hurting each other!"

I had heard nothing of forgiveness, concern or understanding. There had been no hint of love or hope. What I had heard was two egocentric individuals trying to get in the last word.

I have come to believe that some people should not be married. Some people, in their present spiritual condition, should not have children. Some people are incapable of creating worthy relationships. They are incapable of true love. In John 15:12, Jesus tells his disciples *to "Love one another as I have loved you."* This is the key to all relationships. The Greek word translated as love is *agape*. It does not mean a romantic or sentimental emotion. It denotes a genuine caring and nurturing activity. When Jesus tells us to love our enemies, for example, he does not mean we must *like* them, or to feel a friendly emotion toward them. He tells us to *care* for them. The Red Cross in combat situations is an example of this *agape*. They do not differentiate between friend or foe

41

in determining if they will care for them. Knowing that they are all God's children they simply tend to those in need.

In 1 Corinthians 13:5, Paul partly defines agape love by telling what it is *not*: *"Love is not rude; it is not self-seeking; it is not easily angered; it keeps no track of wrongs."* Without agape our own egocentricity eventually will destroy any relationship. Egocentric anger will destroy romantic love and friendly love. We will nurture our hurts; count up the wrongs committed; and insist on our own way. We will be unable to forgive and forget. However, agape love is the love of God and cannot be destroyed. Furthermore, agape love and self-centered anger cannot dwell together. If you possess that kind of Godly love it will drive out the anger from within you, and you will find yourself able to forgive and forget the inevitable hurts and disappointments all relationships generate.

Part of the problem in "letting go" is that we may find a strange comfort in these ill feelings. They become like old friends. We may experience some unhealthy pleasure in feeling like a victim or in plotting revenge. We may enjoy the sense of self-righteousness the memories elicit. In short we may already have given the devil a foothold, and have diminished ourselves in the process.

Agape is not simply an emotion. It must take action. Agape might even develop from a decision. We *resolve* to be charitable, to display human kindness and generosity. In effect, we choose to be what Jesus calls us to be. Agape may begin as an act of the will. It ends as an attribute of the soul.

There was another couple whose marriage was in crisis. The husband was quite successful in his work. Perhaps he had been too successful. A great deal of his time and energy had gone into his professional life, leaving little time for his private life. Somewhere along the way, an emotional separation occurred. The wife, feeling unneeded and unwanted, became prey to a young man. They had an affair. Then she decided to abandon her husband and live with her new lover. As I said, she was only his *prey*, not really his lover. When he had spent what money she had, he threw her out. Devastated and desperate, she had nowhere to turn... but home. When she entered the door, she saw her husband sitting in the living room. She stood quietly…afraid and embarrassed…not knowing what to say, or what to do. Then her husband noticed her. He hesitated for just a moment, observing her pathetic state, and realizing that he had, in some way he did not yet understand, contributed to this ordeal. Then he walked toward her, arms out-stretched; tenderly took her in his arms; and quietly whispered to her: "Since you and I have done this thing together, let us now see how *together* we might put us back together."

He, of course, had suffered greatly. His concern, however, was for this woman he had once committed himself to love, "for better or for worse." Agape at work eventually created forgiveness and wholeness for both parties.

If we choose to forgive and forget there actually is a means for accomplishing it. Memory follows a path. Some paths are well-worn, but even these can be redrawn in other directions. I discover that when my mind starts to wander down some pathway I do not choose to follow, I can simply turn its direction to a more worthy destination. Let me return, once more, to my feud at the academy. Today, if my mind begins to trace that once well-worn path, I simply change its course. I look at myself at that time, and realize how I contributed to the problem. I gently chide myself for that foolishness, look at the hard-learned lesson I received, and let it go. God desires that we learn from our failures, not that we suffer from their memory.

In the early days of my ministry I had the opportunity to attend a retreat in which Joe Yeakle was the leader. Joe was later to become a bishop, but at this time he was just, "Joe". He told a group of us about an experience he had in his first parish. A young teenager from his church crashed his car, killing his girlfriend. Joe spoke to the boy, comforting him, but also told him he must go to his girlfriend's family. The young man did not want to go, so Joe accompanied him as far as the front doorstep. Joe described the scene vividly.

The house was typical of most Pennsylvania mining towns. It was wooden, plain, in need of some repairs. The front door was two steps up, but they were giant steps, with just one thin strip of cement to balance oneself on while waiting for the door to be opened. The young man stood there, teetering on the step, waiting nervously for someone to answer his knock. When the door opened , the girl's father appeared. He was a giant of a man. His face was dark with grief. As he looked down at the trembling young man, his face became contorted with an obviously painful emotion. He bent over and lifted the boy from the door stoop to where their noses practically touched. The boy just hung in his arms like a limp rag doll. Joe stood transfixed, wondering what might happen next. Then the father struggled through his pain to slowly speak these words: "Billy, no matter what you might think - no matter what you may hear . . . *I forgive you.*"

Joe told us it was at that moment when he truly understood the message of the cross, "*Father, forgive them, for they know not what they do.*" (Luke 23:34) . . . and God did forgive. . . and continues to forgive. God simply lets it go . . . and we are told, "*Beloved, if God so loved us, we ought to love one another.*"   (I John 4:11)

REFLECTIONS

It is our egos - our egocentricities - which require retribution, which distort the meaning of justice to become synonymous with vengeance. Our ego represents that portion of us which is consciously aware. It establishes our personal boundaries, setting us apart from all others. A strong ego is essential to our development as a human being. Without a strong, well-defined ego we may become mere reflections of what others desire us to be - figments of other's imaginations. I have observed weak egos begging others upon whom they are dependent to, "Tell me what you want me to be." These weak egos are easily led astray, and are easily overrun and manipulated. Our genuine selves, however, this Image-of-God in whom we are made, is far more than our conscious selves - far more than our little egos. This is the "Christ-consciousness," the God within, of whom Jesus speaks in John 14:23:

If anyone loves me he will keep my word and the Father will love him, and come to him, and make his abode with him.

Within every ego there is a warrior whose task is to protect and provide for the whole person. The young, immature inner-warrior must accept every challenge. It is only when the warrior within us matures that he or she will be able to discern the battles worth fighting. Because of my affection for the first cadet, my warrior chose not to do battle. This was a sign of emerging maturity. However, when confronted by the officer in my own room, the young, immature warrior came forth and *engaged the enemy*. I was seventeen years old, and had to travel much farther before I could select my battles more carefully.

The couple whose bitter marriage ended so dreadfully, had locked themselves in a combat of egos wherein each found it necessary to justify his or her own actions by projecting all the blame on the other. They let their inner warriors dominate the relationship. The more caring, more rational parts within each were submerged, inactive, and ineffective. They had no ability to check for the log in their own eye. Rather, they had reverted to the rules of Leviticus, of an eye for an eye. Tragically, too many self-professed Christians may call Jesus Lord, Lord, but not do as he says.

Questions for Reflection and Discussion

1. What was the key difference between the author's first conflict with a fellow cadet, and the second conflict with a faculty officer?

2. What might he have done differently both times?

3. How might different reactions have created different results?

4. Have you ever found yourself in the position of carrying a grudge or continuing a feud? Do you relate to the author's experience of carrying a grudge? If so, how did you handle it? How did (or might) you change that to something positive?

5. What ongoing feuds or needless rivalries do we have in our society?

6. What are key elements in learning to let go of anger, perceived injustices, old injuries?

7. What other passages of Scripture might you have brought to one of these situations?

SCRIPTURE REFERENCES

Matthew 5:17 Think not that I have come to abolish the law and the prophets; I have come not to abolish them but to fulfill them.

Matthew 5: 38-39 You have heard that it was said, "an eye for an eye and a tooth for a tooth." But I say to you do not resist one who is evil. But if anyone hits you on your right cheek turn to him the other also.

Luke 6:46: Why do you call me, "Lord, Lord," and not do what I tell you?

Luke 23:34 Father, forgive them, for they know not what they do.

John 15:12 This is my commandment that you love one another as I have loved you.

Romans 12:17 Do not repay evil for evil. Try always to do what is right in the eyes of everyone.

Romans 12:21 Do not overcome evil with evil, but overcome evil with good.

I Corinthians 13:5b Love does not insist on its own way; it is not irritable or resentful.

I Corinthians 13:11 When I was a child I spoke like a child, I thought like a child, I reasoned like a child; when I became a man I gave up childish ways.

Philippians 3:12 Not that I have already attained this or am already perfect; but I press on to make it my own, because Christ Jesus has made me his own.

Ephesians 4:26 Be angry but do not sin; do not let the sun go down on your anger, and do not give the devil a foothold.

I John 4:11 Beloved, if God so loved us we ought to love one another.

5. LEARNING TO LOVE

It promised to be a rewarding summer. The twelve week Pastoral Clinical Training program at the University of Michigan would provide twelve more credits, while allowing me to live at home in nearby Napoleon, Michigan. Further, it would help me to meet the requirements for my honors concentration in pastoral psychology, while giving me some useful tools for my ministry. So far as I could see it was a Win - Win situation.

As things turned out I was correct, but not in the manner I had imagined.

My supervisor was the senior hospital chaplain, Malcom Balinger. I do not know whether Malcom still walks this earth. If he does I hope he encounters this remembrance of my days with him. For that summer was not only a turning point in my life, but the most powerful single learning experience I had while in seminary.

There were thirteen seminarians in the class. We were a motley crew of various denominations. At age thirty-five I was the obvious elder of the group.

We spent our first two weeks serving as orderlies. Malcom believed this gave us a candid peek at patients when we were not wearing our little white jacket with the cross sewn upon it. We were soon to discover that orderlies are essentially invisible to patients, and that patients tend to behave quite differently when a doctor or chaplain is present. Prior to learning this important fact, however, I was upset by having this lowly task thrust upon me. I was a graduate student, studying pastoral psychology. I was there to serve as a chaplain, not a bedpan commando.

As things turned out it was in this servant role that some of my greatest learning took place.

Somewhere in my studies of the Gospels I must have overlooked Jesus' statement that *"Whoever wishes to become great among you must be your servant."* (Mark 10:44)

We were given about an hour of basic orientation and then turned loose in the wards as orderlies. No one in the wards was to know that we actually were chaplain interns in disguise. However, the nurses were familiar with the hospital's routine, so when a group of well-scrubbed, inept orderlies appeared they quickly had us pegged. I assumed that none of the patients would recognize who we were, which gave me mixed feelings. I half hoped they would recognize that we did not belong in such menial roles.

Again, I was correct but not in the manner I had wanted.

I was given the task of changing a patient's bed sheets. Since I had been to a military academy I had long known how to change and make up a bed. However this particular one posed a special problem. There was an elderly man lying in it. As I sauntered toward him I assumed that I could handle this simply by making up one side, then rolling him over to that side while making up the other. This may or may not have been the correct procedure. Fortunately I was never given the opportunity to make another attempt. However, something in my general plan must have been lacking some critical details. It quickly became obvious to me that I had no idea what I was doing, and was only succeeding in disturbing this elderly patient. Fortunately, I thought, he had no idea that I was totally confused, so I continued puttering with the sheets in some vain attempt to finally get that bed made and get out of there with some sense of decorum still intact. Then, quite unexpectedly, the man sat up and got out of the bed. Relieved, I hastily completed my task. As I was doing so he gave me a smile of encouragement and said, "Don't worry, you'll get the hang of it." Then he proceeded to tell me that he had been an employee of this hospital during his working years. He appreciated how difficult it was to learn all the little techniques necessary for the job.

Of all the people to practice on, I had to pick the one professional who would realize I was a rank amateur, totally unaware of what I was doing. His kindness and affirmation humbled me even further. He could have chosen to be gruff and critical of "this younger generation." But he did not. He was gentle and helpful. Further, without even trying he had taught me that even this "menial job" required skills I did not possess. *You* count the lessons from this episode.

Shortly after this, one of the other elderly men in the ward wanted a bath. Fortunately they had a private tub for this task, and I did not need to repeat my earlier performance publicly - this time with a wet sponge. I assisted him to the bathroom, drew his tub, helped him into the bath, and began to bathe him. As I sponged him gently, and he luxuriated in the warmth of the water, we began to chat. He told me of his younger days when he and his wife were building their lives together. They had adopted a daughter, an older girl who had not been placed by her orphanage because of her age. There had been a difficult adjustment period, but eventually she had become their daughter in fact, and had proved to be a joy to them. Then he mentioned that they had always worked hard, rarely taking vacations. There were just too many things which required their attention in those days, he believed. "We figured we would travel and enjoy ourselves when we retired, " he said. Then there was a pause, and he continued wistfully "but it looks as though we may never have that retirement together." I knew that to be true because I had learned before bathing him that he had terminal cancer.

I would offer no words of false encouragement. That would have been trite and demeaning to him. It was not yet time for me to step out of the phone booth and don my super chaplain coat. Even if it had been, I seriously doubt that I would have been able to find the words to speak to his spiritual needs. The only comfort I could offer him at that moment was to keep his bath water warm and soak him with the sponge. So I added the water and kept bathing him as gently as I could. I felt then, and still feel, a deep compassion for that gentle spirit whom I barely knew.

In the large ward there were two young men bedded next to each other. I assumed this was intentional to allow them some sort of companionship. The year, however, was 1965, and one of the young men, Matthew, was black. The other, Bill, was white. Their different races seemed totally irrelevant to them. The interpersonal chemistry was great! Matthew needed open heart surgery to repair a faulty valve. This was a very delicate and risky surgical procedure in those days. On the morning of the scheduled surgery Bill prayed with Matthew. I joined them as an orderly friend. Bill, whose problem gave him great difficulty in moving, insisted on going to the family waiting room. After the operation he went to the surgical intensive care unit to visit Matthew, even though he remained unconscious. One day Bill returned in tears. Matthew had died. Bill was heart-sick, and mourned the death of his new friend as though they had been life-long buddies. Bill would leave the hospital in a few weeks and continue his life as he had before he met - and lost - Matthew. However, he would, I realized, carry a silent ache somewhere in his heart for some time to come. The words of a childhood hymn arose in my mind. "*What wondrous love is this, O my soul.*" I thought it wondrously strange that a person could care so deeply for another in so short a time.

And I realized I had much yet to learn on my journey.

One very clear and powerful understanding which resulted from my work in that crowded ward was the realization that the patients genuinely cared for one another. They became a mini-healing community. Many struggled to get to the bedside of an almost total stranger in order to give some degree of comfort. This was a sight I was not to witness again once I left the wards to become a chaplain.

After the two week orientation, we were given our white jackets and assigned as chaplains to specific areas of the hospital. Although I was eager to "get on with the training," I felt a twinge of sadness in departing the wards and the people who, curiously, had become very important to me.

Since I was a product of the suburbs I was assigned to one of the two floors with private rooms rather than the wards. This was before

51

health insurance had made wards a thing of the past. One patient was an affable man about my age. He recently had switched careers, as had I, and had become established in it, as I was becoming established in mine. He was married with two children, as was I. We appeared to have a lot in common. So I thought, until I learned of his condition. He had an incurable heart problem that would kill him. In fact it was in the process of taking his life, which is why he was there.

Something began to occur within me that I simply could not understand. I found myself not wanting to visit him. He was bright and interesting. His wife, who usually was present, was attractive and gracious. Yet I caught myself planning to see him at times when I knew the nurses would be present and attending to his physical needs, giving us little time for conversation. I would bounce in, say a few words, and bounce out, unable to attend to his spiritual needs because of the busyness and confusion. Later in my scheduled supervisory sessions Malcom helped me to understand what was happening. In effect I had overly-related to the patient. I experienced a combination of guilt and fear every time I visited him. I felt guilty because I was healthy and he was not. I went home to my family every night. He never would. I had a bright future. He had no future. On the other side of the ledger some part of me understood that if this could happen to him it could just as easily happen to *me*. Every time I saw him a part of myself was reminded of this fact, and wished to avoid it. I cared for him. Certainly I did! However I cared more deeply for *myself*. This self-concern interfered with my ability to help him in his time of need.

Malcom added a word of assurance to our discussion. I believe he meant it as assurance. However, its effect was like that of a double-edged sword. "Don't worry about your patients, Dick. We are following behind picking up the pieces. Your task is to become better at pastoral care. Ours is to care for the patients' needs." The staff understood that we interns were unable to deal with many of the situations we would encounter, and were following behind cleaning up our messes. Like John Wesley in Georgia, I who had come to bring salvation to the natives, discovered I was in need of salvation, myself.

It was a terrible revelation!   It was a wonderful revelation!

It thrust me into the wilderness of my soul, where amidst tears and fears, I searched for fresh understanding of the complexity of which we are comprised. Our self-concern literally gets in the way of relationships! Even when we believe we genuinely are concerned for someone else we may just be playing peek-a-boo with our souls. A deeper part of us may be monitoring the situation and asking, "Am I making a good impression?" or "Could this ever happen to me?" Perhaps Jesus was addressing this dynamic when he said we had to lose our lives in order to find them.

He called the crowd with his disciples, and said to them, "If any of you would be my followers, let them deny themselves, and take up their cross, and follow me. For those who want to save their life will lose it and those who lose their life for my sake and the sake of the Gospel will save it." (Mark 8:34-35)

Just before the summer session mercifully drew to its close a member of my congregation asked me to visit a friend of hers in another hospital. She informed me that her friend had a terminal illness but was unable to talk about it. Perhaps I could help? I shall never forget that visit. I stood at the door, spoke her name, and then introduced myself. "Alice asked me drop in to see you," I offered by way of explanation for my unexpected appearance. "Come in," she replied. "How are you doing?" I inquired as I made my way to her bedside. "Not well," she responded. "Why not? What's happening?" I asked as I stood beside her. "I'm dying," she replied. It was just that easy. No hesitation. I asked an honest question. She answered honestly. We talked about what this dying business meant to her. We mourned the approaching loss of family and friends. We discussed her religious convictions of life beyond life. We held hands, and we prayed. She seemed relieved and contented with what we had shared. I left her room feeling far better than when I had entered.

On my trip home I reflected upon what had transpired. Alice was a wise and compassionate person. She and her friends had been unable to penetrate the surface veneers which keep us separated from one another. Somewhere in my summer internship I had been stripped of the normal defenses we utilize to protect ourselves from painful involvement with

53

others. There are a number of ways of inquiring about people's well-being which preclude honest answers. I had witnessed any number of "cheery visitors" with family members or friends whose condition did not warrant such cheerfulness. I had observed too many visitors making diversionary small talk while the patient - surrounded by "loved ones" - lay quietly dying . . . alone.

As I stated earlier, we begin with self-centeredness and then either move away from that condition, or we become more entrenched with ourselves. The Greek word, *krisis*, means judgment. We tend to think of a crisis as being a moment of confusion or chaos. It actually is a moment of critical decision. After the crisis a situation either improves or worsens. In our moments of crisis we reveal who we are and in which direction we have moved through life. *Agape* (caring love) opportunities become moments of crisis. In that area of loving, many of us are still found wanting.

A giant step in this journey of understanding Christian love came from one of my professors of preaching, Dr. George Buttrick. He noted that the much-loved passage, John 3:16, invariably was mistranslated as *"For God so loved the world that he gave his only begotten son that those believing in Him should not perish but have everlasting life."* He then proceeded to explain why he believed this to be so. I will share his explanation. First I will give a transliteration of the Greek, then I will place the literal English translation beneath each word. The Greek sentence structure is a bit different from ours, so bear with me. The key word is the first in the sentence.

Outos gar egapesen ho theos ton cosmon oste ton huion ton
Thus for loved the God the world so as the son the

monogene edoken hina pas ho pisteuon eis auton
only-begotten he gave in order that all the ones believing into him

me apoletai all' exe zoen aionion
not perish but may have life eternal.

54

For those who did not read Greek Dr. Buttrick explained that the term *"outos"* can be translated as "so." However, it means "so" in the sense of "thus" or "in this manner." If John 3:16 is read with this understanding it states quite clearly that God's love is an action not just an emotion which may beget an action. Read it again with this translation, *"For thus (in this manner) God loved the world in that he gave his only-begotten son that all those believing in Him would not perish but may have life eternal."*

Agape love *necessitates* acting on behalf of the beloved.

Years later, while studying the passages in John 21:15-17 in Greek, I picked up another new understanding. You know the scene. A group of disciples are fishing in the early morning. Jesus comes to the beach, builds a fire, places some fish on the coals, then calls to them. When the disciples figure out who he is they rush to the shore to greet him. After the fish fry Jesus takes Peter aside and asks him, "Do you love me?" There are various words which we translate as "love." *Philia* means friendly affection as in Philadelphia, "Brotherly love." *Agape* is a more complex term. It once was translated as "charity" when "love" was considered too suggestive of romance and lust. As I explained earlier it is far more than an emotion. It is a dynamic which blends a caring concern which necessarily includes active manifestation of that emotion (as in John 3:16). John's recounting of the conversation between Jesus and Peter plays upon the distinction between these two forms of love. In the first exchange Jesus asks Peter, "Do you *agape* me?" Peter responds, "Lord, you know I *philia* you. The second exchange repeats the first. Jesus asks for *agape*. Peter expresses *philia*. The third time around Jesus changes the verb. He asks simply, "Do you *philia* me?" Peter apparently not recognizing the difference, becomes impatient with the question, but responds once more time, "Lord, you know everything. You *know* that I *philia* you." Jesus met Peter where he was.

There is a time in our lives when we have no idea what *agape* really means. *Philia* is all we understand. It is all we are capable of giving. If life is kind we learn agape love from those who have received it and passed it along. Christ ultimately meets us where we are in our capacity to love. He offers the invitation and we can either accept it or ignore it, and continue our self-centered way. Peter accepted. Obviously somewhere along the way agape became second nature to him.

REFLECTIONS

As I reflect upon this life-long endeavor of learning to love I realize the profound truth to John's statement, "*We love because He first loved us.* (1 John 4:19). It is through the actions of real, live people that we experience God's love most vividly. For us Christians there is a two-fold pattern for our loving. We see the way in which Jesus expressed God's love to society, and we set this as our conscious example. We also have witnessed those who have modeled their lives after Christ and have made that love flesh and blood in our own lives. We have been nurtured, accepted, comforted, guided, forgiven, and assisted along life's path by a multitude of personal saints, many who now are but blurred memories. Yet their lessons of love remain embedded somewhere in our souls. Our life experiences teach us ways in which we can and should love one another. I believe that if we were to examine our personal love histories closely we would see that we tend to imitate the styles in which we have been loved in meaningful ways.

My journey has also taught me that we can learn and practice new ways of loving. There are activities we can undertake which can move us away from self-preoccupation into the dimension of Christian love.

Intercessory prayer pulls us from self-concern toward the greater needs of others whose needs are more profound, more worthy of our concern.

Active participation as a volunteer whose task calls for serving others helps us to break the barriers we have erected to keep the uncomfortable parts of the world outside ourselves.

Donating money and property to worthy causes or to help meet the needs of others is another method for razing the barriers we have erected to protect ourselves from the stark realities of life. In many respects we are like the rich man who asked Jesus for the secret to eternal life

(Mark 10:17-22). Surrounded by wealth most of the world cannot even imagine, we insulate ourselves from our own humanity. Giving of this wealth helps to draw us into an arena where truly great and good things are happening.

The question may remain: Why should I, or you, or anyone desire to lose our egocentricity and become more involved in the lives of others? It requires sacrifice of effort, time, money, and other personal resources we could spend upon ourselves. The only answer I can give is that in those moments of involvement we feel more in touch with that which is genuine and worthy. We lose ourselves and our petty concerns. We find these experiences more satisfying than any of the many diversions and pastimes we use to fill up our otherwise empty days.

As I look back upon this chapter I would try to answer a few unspoken questions you may have:

Have I cut myself free from my own egocentricity and entered fully into this experience of agape? No, not by a long shot, but I am working on it. My inner caregiver is alive and well, but still has a long way to go.

Am I making progress in that direction? I hope so . . . I really hope so.

QUESTIONS FOR REFLECTION AND DISCUSSION

1. What are your feelings (and reactions) when visiting someone with a serious illness, at a funeral home, or some other difficult situation?

2. A slogan the author learned during his clinical training was, "Words conceal; they don't reveal." What does that mean? How do people use words "to conceal?" How have you found yourself using words to conceal?"

3. What are the crucial differences between agape love and philia love?

4. Do you share feelings of regret for missed opportunities which required more love than you were capable of giving at the time? If so, what can you do about it?

5. How do we develop compassion for people we barely know?

SCRIPTURAL REFERENCES

Matthew 25:40 And the king will answer them, "Truly, I say to you, as you did it to the least of these, my brethren, you did it to me."

Mark 8:34-35 He called the crowd with his disciples, and said to them, "If any of you would be my followers, let them deny themselves, and take up their cross, and follow me. For those who want to save their life will lose it and those who lose their life for my sake and the sake of the Gospel will save it."

Mark 10: 21-22 And Jesus looking upon him loved him, and said to him, "You lack one thing; go sell what you have and give it to the poor, and you will have treasures in heaven, and come follow me." At that saying his countenance fell, and he went away sorrowful, for he had great possessions.

Mark 10:44 . . . and whoever would be first among you must be servant to all.

John 3:16 For thus (in this manner) God loved the world in that he gave his only-begotten son that all those believing in him would not perish but may have life eternal.

John 21: 15-17 When they had finished breakfast Jesus said to Simon Peter, "Simon son of John, do you love me more than these?" He said to him, "Yes, Lord, you know that I love you." He said to him, "Feed my lambs." A second time he said to him, "Simon, son of John, do you love me?" He said to him, "Yes, Lord, you know that I love you." He said to him, "Tend my sheep." He said to him a third time, "Simon, son of John, do you love me?" Peter was grieved because he said to him a third time, "Do you love me?" And he said to him, "Lord, you know everything; you know that I love you." Jesus said to him, "Feed my sheep."

I Corinthians 13: 4-8a Love is patient and kind; love is not jealous or boastful; it is not arrogant or rude. Love does not insist on its own way; it is not irritable or resentful; it does not rejoice at the wrong but rejoices in the right. Love bears all things, believes all things, hopes all things, endures all things. Love never ends.

Philippians 3:12 Not that I have already obtained all this or have been made perfect; but I press on to take hold of that for which Christ Jesus took hold of me.

James 1:23 . . . those who hear but do not care are like those looking in a mirror. Compare with 1 Corinthians 13:12 . . . now we see in a mirror darkly.

James 4:17 Anyone who knows the right thing to do and does not do it commits a sin. (more properly translated, Anyone who knows the right thing to do and does not do it, that is a failing.).

I John 4:18 There is no fear in love; but perfect love casts out fear. For fear has to do with punishment, and he who fears is not perfected in love.

I John 4:19 We love because he first loved us.

6. JOYFUL REPENTANCE

We were compatriots, reasonably young and idealistic. We were clergy in Ann Arbor, Michigan during those marvelously tumultuous years of the 70's. One Presbyterian (Bob), one Episcopalian (Richard), and one Methodist (me). We were non-traditionalists, serving new congregations in the expanding portion of the city. During one of our "how to change the world" pow wows I found myself playing intellectual tug-of-war with Bob. Actually, it was Richard who noticed the budding debate. "What's going on here?" he inquired. "I thought you two were pretty much alike in your theology." Bob put his finger on the issue first. "I can't agree with Dick's use of the word, 'Repent,'" he said. "To me this suggests that the person already is heading for hell. That condemns him, and I can't do that." "That's your residual Calvinism," I chided. "I come from Wesley and see repent as a good word. Jesus would not have called people to repent if they were not capable of doing so."

Having given this intuitive response I stepped back to take another look at this dynamic we call repentance. I recalled that my initial understanding of the term called for contrition. I dimly remembered some revival-style experiences from my childhood. People came to the altar railing, heavily burdened with tears in their eyes. They seemed to agonize as they knelt and wept their tears of remorse. I no longer understood repentance solely in that terrible, negative way. Somewhere along the way my perception had changed. I embarked on a quest to better understand repentance in order to see how it fell into the grand scheme of our faith. I also desired to learn how my own understanding had changed so dramatically. From the start I realized that this excursion was going to be a "head trip," an intellectual pursuit. I would be trying to assist my mind in catching up with my soul. What I was to learn would be both enlightening and personally redemptive. It also was a bit disheartening.

For years I had heard that repent simply meant "turn around." It was the theme of many sermons: "Turn around and find the Kingdom." I decided it was time to check out the term for myself. Actually the Greek word we translate as repent means something quite different. It is *metanoia*. A quick and easy translation of this means "change your mind" (which may or may not result in changing one's direction). A more careful examination of the word suggests something far more profound. In Mark 9:2 the term used to describe Jesus' transfiguration is *metamorphothe*. Let's look at the root meaning of the two terms which make up this word: *meta* and *morphos*. When joined together they indicate a transformation of the body. *(morphos)*. When *meta* is joined with *noia* translators tend to call it a *change of mind*. Now it is true that a change is a transformation. However, the connotation is quite different. We change our minds all the time. Rarely, if ever, do we *transform* them. Also, the term noia or nous embraces the concepts of perception and understanding. It refers to far more than a linear thought process. In the Greek *metanoia* also conveys the understanding that this transformation begins after reflective consideration. This was the first century's understanding of the term: Reflect upon your life, then radically change your mind - transform your way of understanding.

Next I checked the dictionary definition of repent. It includes a sense of regret as a necessary ingredient. This differs from the original Greek meaning of the word, and it differs from my own observation and experience. Certainly I have seen people moved to radically change their lives because of a strong sense of regret or anger. I have also witnessed those whose decision to change arose from a feeling of inner emptiness. They were somewhat like the rich young man who approached Jesus seeking the formula for eternal life (Matthew 19:16-22). These people, however, did not let their possessions interfere with their inner hunger. They repented. They developed a fresh outlook on life. I have also walked with those who seemed to have passed through an invisible curtain into another, deeper dimension of life. Perhaps it came upon them at a spiritual retreat. Perhaps it arose from some

61

reflective moment of lucidity. Whatever precipitated it they felt a sense of wholeness and serenity which transcended any previous experience. Repentance for them was a burning desire to live their lives more fully in this newly experienced dimension. Their only regret, if any, was that they had been so long in discovering the possibility of a new life. Remorse never was a primary ingredient in most of the repentance -or conversion - experiences I have witnessed. I believe the typical pilgrim is more attracted to that which promises renewal and joy than in fleeing from pain and regret.

I reflected upon my early days as a preacher. My congregants often met me with a smile at the conclusion of the service, saying, "You really gave it to us today, pastor." I took this as a compliment thinking I had done what I was supposed to do in a sermon. This was the model I had for preaching. Hit them hard enough with guilt and they were sure to want to change their lives. Somewhere in the inner recesses of my soul, however, this just did not seem right. These people were essentially fine and decent. I was causing them to feel guilty and for some strange reason they seemed to appreciate it when I did. I suppose this was when I began my journey of reflective contemplation and the long, arduous process of transforming the way I thought.

In my repentance I rediscovered the Gospel.

The Jesus I knew proclaimed Good News. Yet through the years the church often has perverted that message into Bad News. We have forgotten the joyful proclamation of the angels to the shepherds. We have forgotten the scriptural proclamation that we were made in God's image. Too often the church has emphasized sin, guilt, judgment, and punishment. I had been caught up in this and found myself proclaiming more bad news than good. It was the prevailing message of my youth and I had accepted it without critical examination. It is what Eric Berne, the founder of Transactional Analysis would have called "being hooked by your critical parent."[1] We all have that inner voice which repeats and passes on the complaints against ourselves and society in general. We play the game "Ain't it a Shame" and talk ourselves into despair. We focus upon the empty portion of the glass and overlook all the good it contains.

In my first parish I spent many evenings in solitary walks through the little village of Napoleon, Michigan. As I navigated the narrow sidewalks along the quiet houses and empty fields I struggled with the question, "What in God's name am I trying to say?" As I passed the homes of many of the parishioners I fleetingly thought of each family that dwelt just behind those walls. They were good people, very loving and accepting of me in my ignorance and pastoral ineptness. They had brought Diane, my daughters, and me into their lives, and had accepted us even before they really knew us. They provided us with a home and a reasonable salary. Why would they do this for a yet-to-be-trained budding pastor? What was it they hoped to receive in return? It could not be the constant reminder of their sinfulness, weaknesses and failures. At least it should not have been those things. They needed to be lifted from those portions of their lives and given hope. Then a very simple but significant transformation began to occur in my thinking. As I reflect upon it today it is so simple and so obvious that I feel foolish in admitting I was not aware of it at that time - that I was more than thirty years of age before it dawned upon my consciousness.

Everything that is stated in a negative manner can
be stated more effectively in a positive framework.

I thought of the negative messages I had received as a child, that had been given to me - that I had heard other parents give to their children. Each one could have been phrased in an affirming manner:

"You are a bad boy/girl!"   "You are better than that."

"If you don't study you will fail" "You can pass if you study harder."

"Can't you do anything right?" "Let's look at why this did not work."

"That was stupid!"   "You can make better choices."

The list is endless. It just requires reflective thought and a change in approach. Instead, many parents cripple their children emotionally, not necessarily out of maliciousness but simply because they pass along, unexamined, the messages embedded in their souls. In some respects

63

the sins (failures) of the parents *really are* visited to the children of the third and fourth generation. So, too, the sins of the church have been visited to ensuing generations of believers. I had been giving the same disapproving messages to the members of my congregation. From that moment of realization I resolved that I would not remain a part of this tacit conspiracy of negativism.

I continued to pursue the long, difficult process of repentance for at least one of my sins. I searched the Scriptures anew. This time I focused upon the abundance of good news which filled the pages. Jesus' essential message is proclaimed quite simply in Mark 1:14: "*The time is fulfilled, and the Kingdom of God is at hand; repent and believe the gospel.*" I interpreted this to mean that Jesus was saying that everything is ready. God's realm is open and waiting. Just transform the way in which you have looked at life; trust this message and become part of God's people! In Luke 17:20-21, Jesus tells the Pharisees to stop looking for magical signs of the coming kingdom. The Greek allows for one of two interpretations of what he says next. The Kingdom is either *in the midst* of you, or it is *within* you. Either interpretation states that Jesus is speaking of a spiritual realm not a physical one. It is a spiritual relationship with God that already is available. It is open to all comers. Paul stated that understanding quite clearly in II Corinthians 5:19: "*In Christ God was reconciling the world to himself, not counting their trespasses against them, and entrusting to us the message of reconciliation.*" Paul says there are no chosen few, no record of wrongs stored up for a final judgment. Further it is our task to share this message of God's graciousness toward all people.

Jesus' radical new teaching was that the spiritual realm is more real than the physical. We are not mere physical creatures who may have an occasional spiritual experience. We are spiritual beings who are undergoing a temporary physical experience. God is not to be viewed as a distant judge or ruler, but as an ever-present loving parent. To understand this we must learn to see with spiritual eyes, hear with spiritual ears, and think with a spiritual mind. In other words we must repent in the true meaning of the word. In Mark 8:18 Jesus chides his followers for worrying about having enough bread just after he had fed

64

about four thousand people with seven loaves of bread: *"Having eyes do you not see, and having ears do you not hear?"*

Have you ever seen one of those trick pictures that actually contains two images within one another? When you first see it the dominant, obvious image appears in your consciousness. However, if you alter your perspective the other image emerges. The second picture is the least familiar of the two. This is what is involved in classic repentance. Perhaps a better illustration would be the picture composed of many colored dots, which at first glance has no image at all. However if you gaze at it with a detached, non-focused stare a three dimensional picture appears. You may excitedly hand it to a friend and give instructions on how to view it. Often your friend hands it back with a negative remark like, "I don't a see a thing," or "You're putting me on." Perhaps this is more akin to the quality of repentance which allows one to view the spiritual dimension of life. For reasons unknown to me some can do it quickly while others have more difficulty and may even give up the effort.

As I continued to reflect upon Jesus' call to repentance it seemed to be a three-pronged demand:

The first requires changing the way of thinking about God. God is to be understood as a loving parent, not an angry judge. Jesus gave us the name, "Father" for God to signify One who is loving and personally involved, yet One who sets the rules and is the ultimate authority for our lives. He taught us that God is more interested in our redemption than our punishment. He also helped us understand that God is neither distant nor naïve. God hears us in our silent thoughts and is not deceived by appearances. This called for a radical transformation of thinking for the people of that day . . . and for many of this day.

The second calls us to develop a totally new perspective on what we deem to be reality. The spiritual preceded the physical and takes precedence over it. Our sciences are just beginning to catch up with that understanding. When I was a child in public school I was taught that matter could neither be created nor destroyed. I was also taught that the atom was the smallest particle of matter, and could not be broken. Now we realize it is not matter but energy which can neither be created nor destroyed. It can only be contained, transformed, or released. Everything which appears to our eyes as solid matter actually is a mass of energy. At our core we are a mass of spiritual energy. We are primarily spiritual beings. Our permanence lies in that realm. "Do not store up treasures on earth, but in heaven," Jesus told his followers (Matthew 6:19-20). He made it clear where we are to spend eternity.

The third prong calls for radically altering our view on the purpose and values of life. Jesus set his premise in his Sermon on the Mount and then continued to challenge the conventional wisdom of his day. He asked people to discard their temporal values and latch on to those of eternal worth. In honesty I have marveled and delighted in his teachings for most of my life. They generate marvelous images and elicit latent idealism. However I realize that I have mostly just *marveled* and *delighted* in them. I rarely considered actually putting them into practice in my daily life. Eventually I realized that if I genuinely believed that Jesus Christ is Lord I must take his teachings more seriously. Jesus had to become the actual guide for my life. His words and His actions must necessarily become my reigning authority. The other writings and characters of Scripture might be useful to aid in my understanding. It must be Jesus, however, who is to take precedence over all other authorities.

What then did Jesus say about the purpose and values of life? What did his actions teach us about these two? The traditionally understood values of life, *e.g.* wealth, success, power, and prestige are temporary and false. The more worthy, more lasting values are love, fidelity, compassion, and justice. Couple the parable of the Final Judgment (Matthew 25:31-40) with that of Lazarus and the rich man (Luke 16:20-31) and it seems clear that Jesus wishes us to understand that when we leave this existence bound by time and space we shall enter a realm in which all relationships are spiritual - not spatial or temporal. The quality of our spiritual relationships carries over into that realm. Nothing else passes the veil. If we live in honest, loving relationships in this life we shall continue in that mode beyond this earthly life. Furthermore, because God is love we shall be in close spiritual relationship with God as we step into eternity. On the other hand if we have separated ourselves from loving involvement in this life, that also shall continue.

I had to ask myself what it is that prevents us from living comfortably and naturally in loving relationships with one another. I recalled a former English professor who continually voiced his pet theory on life. "Man's greatest need is to appear well in the eyes of his peers." Then he would elaborate, relating instances when a person sacrificed himself in some way in order to appear courageous, gentlemanly, or the like. I argued this point with him, contending that our greatest need is to appear well in our own eyes - or mind. We want to think kindly of ourselves. We need to believe we are decent and worthy. To do this we often play peek-a-boo with our souls, denying our true motives and projecting our baser parts onto others. I eventually accepted both his and my own premise. Some of us are more inner-directed. Some of us are more other-directed. We all require some positive feedback from others. To the extent that we are dependent upon others for our self-image, then to that degree - and only to that degree - do we need to appear well in the eyes of others.

This need leads us to avoid genuine intimacy with others. We are as Jesus called the Pharisees, "hypocrites." We are as actors hiding behind our role masks. The slogan I learned in clinical training is too true: "Words conceal they do not reveal." We select our words to generate the image we wish to project. Many of what we believe are free choices actually are determined by our need to present the proper image. We can see this most clearly in teenagers, whose need to be accepted and admired usually goes with the territory. They must wear the latest fashion. They must see the "in" movie. They must have the top-of-the-charts CDs. The list is endless. For them these things are requirements, not options. The need to be accepted determines what they probably believe are their free choices. Remember, this is but a handy example. The real subject is *us* and many of *our* not-so-free choices.

Jesus blew away the concept that people are worthy or unworthy based upon their externals. He dined with the outcasts of society, showing his acceptance of them. He also berated the higher classes for their hypocrisy. He placed truth and meaning above security. He rated compassion and humility over power and prestige. He warned about storing up earthly treasures in lieu of spiritual ones. In short Jesus challenged and would have us discard many of the values and goals of life you and I once held (and perhaps still hold) in our heart of hearts.

I reflected upon my years in private business. My goals were wrapped up in profits and prestige. I really believed that I was serving the needs of my family when I was able to provide more things for my wife and daughters. My life goals were to purchase a nicer, larger home in a more upscale location, to own a better automobile, and join some significant yacht or country club. I wanted to be able to provide my family with fine clothes and all the gadgets that serve to make lifer easier and more interesting. I honestly believed that if I was able to accomplish all these things my life would be a success.

If someone were to ask me who I was, I would have named my various roles: businessman, husband, father, amateur musician. If they had asked *how* I was I would have run a mental inventory of my various activities. No matter how they were faring I probably would have responded, "Just fine!" If they had asked me the old Wesley question, "How does it go with your soul?" I might just have stared blankly, wondering what they meant.

Were I to have made an honest inventory of my soul I might have realized that a large portion of my life was spent in diversions, in passing time rather than using it. Much of what passed for conversation was really chit chat. It generated a sense of connection rather than actually building genuine, caring relationships. Rarely had I ever attempted to share the inner part of myself that would reveal my true values, my desires, my frailties and fears. These were kept hidden even from myself.

Then one summer's day as I finished spreading weed and feed on my lawn, a burning question arose within me: "Is this how my life is to be lived? Am I going to try to earn a bundle of money, buy an upscale home, own some nice cars, join a few clubs, have a few laughs, and keep the weeds out of my lawn so the neighbors will smile benevolently upon me?"

I believe it was at that instant that the first nascent movement of repentance began for me. Some silent portion of my soul hungered to be real. I did not just want to pass the time. I wanted to *fill* the time with something of value. I needed my life to have depth and purpose. It should not be only Shakespeare's "tale told by an idiot, full of sound and fury . . .signifying nothing." It was at this moment I began to turn away from my old values and my old ways, and began to turn in earnest toward Jesus Christ.

In my new profession as a minister I soon learned that the same old desires and demands continued. Clergy worry as much about success and its trimmings as anyone else. We also continue to struggle with those frightened, broken inner parts which, if I may paraphrase Paul, keep us from doing the good we would do, and cause us to do the evil we abhor. (Romans 7:19). Somewhere in the ensuing verses (24-25) Paul gives us the key: "*Wretched person that I am. Who will rescue me from this body of death? Thanks be to God through Jesus Christ our Lord.*" The words of Paul written to the congregation at Philippi leaped into my consciousness: "I can do all things through the one who empowers me." (Phil. 4:13)

I discovered remnants of old defenses left over from childhood. These had to be healed if I were to be an effective spokesperson for Christ. One by one I had to sort through these old defensive mechanisms and move them out of the way. They really no longer served any useful purpose. They were just counter-productive habitual ways of thinking and acting. I quickly realized that entering the ministry did not dull my drive for success at all. It merely redirected it. With Christ as my guide I began to redefine the meaning for success, to strip it of its normal criteria. Success in ministry had to focus upon the spiritual growth of the people, not on the size and status of the church. Yet unresolved issues from childhood continued to emerge in new forms. The list went on and on. Look at your own list of inner demons and you will have some idea of mine.

This is where I pause in this chapter of my diary. This is where my struggle remains. Some buttons still are out of place. I continue to discover new areas in need of transformation. I've learned to work on one change at a time, drawing from the strength and guidance of Christ as I go. Immediate, total transformation is well outside my grasp. I would simply sit down by the side of the road and give up the journey if I attempted to deal with every issue at one time. Each small step - each little act of repentance - nevertheless brings an accompanying sense of joy. I've learned that as I proceed in my pilgrimage I encounter old issues recurring at a once-hidden level of my being. In some ways this portion of the journey resembles a spiral road, circling a mountain. I find myself returning to the same area. This time around, however, I observe it from a higher level. Issues I thought had been resolved - totally transformed - put to rest - are met again, and must be navigated anew. This time, however, I have more understanding and more resources for facing them.

I have no idea how high the mountain reaches, or precisely where the road leads. I only know that with Jesus Christ as my companion and guide I must continue to climb upwards.

1 For a fuller understanding of the critical parent I suggest you read Eric Berne's *Games People Play: The Psychology of Human Relationships.* Grove Press, Inc. 1964

REFLECTIONS

Carl Jung has called the mind the logos portion of our being, but claims the soul is the agricultural portion. By this he means that our mind quickly grasps an idea, but it requires a great amount of time for the soul to integrate the idea into itself, to grow and to heal. I believe that, although the mind may quickly grasp an idea, it will revert back to its original state until the soul from which it springs has reshaped itself. This is why New Year's resolutions are soon neglected, and why Sunday's eye-opening sermon seems mundane by Monday. Repentance requires discipline and patience. Plato believed the mind could redeem the soul. Early Christian Gnostics also believed this. Jesus' statement that those who continued in his word would come to know the truth, and that truth would make them free (John 8:31) suggests that Jesus, himself, believed this to be true. Otherwise, why did he spend his time as a rabbi - a teacher? The mind does not begin to have the power of the soul, but it is a primary tool for affecting the soul. John Wesley offered a four-fold system for doing theology: Scripture, Tradition, Experience, and Reason. Throughout all of these, the mind is the dominant tool for interpreting Scripture, Tradition, and even Experience. This is the reason that Jesus called for Repentance as the basis for entering the Kingdom. There does appear to be a Catch 22 aspect to this, however, in that the mind reflects its source: The Soul. In this regard a decisive factor is Love. Love has the capacity to alter one's perspective and priorities. Lovers of God will become what they were created to become. They will do so - not from fear or self-interest - but simply to please the One they love. That is why understanding faith as relationship is crucial.

QUESTIONS FOR REFLECTION AND DISCUSSION

1. What do you think of the author's definition of repentance?

2. Do you see repentance as a joyful or mournful experience?

3. What factors have caused - or could cause - such a repentance in your life?

4. The author states that there are three areas that usually require repentance:
> a. The view of God as Judge.
> b. The view of ultimate reality as physical.
> c. Our goals and values in general.

Are you open to accepting this change in your thinking?

5. Have you made an honest inventory of your soul? What bad news resides there?

6. Where are you in your pilgrimage?

7. What would you like to work on first?

Scriptural References

Mark 1:14   *Now after John was arrested, Jesus came into Galilee, preaching the gospel of God, and saying, the time is fulfilled, and the kingdom of God is at hand; repent and believe the good news.*

Matthew 7:28 And when Jesus finished these sayings, the crowds were astonished at his teachings, for he taught them as one having authority, and not as the scribes.

Matthew 6:19-20 Do not lay up for yourselves treasures on earth, where moth and rust consume and where thieves break in and steal, but lay up for yourselves treasures in heaven, where neither moth nor rust consume, and where thieves do no break in and steal. For where your treasure is there will your heart be also.

Matthew 25:40 And the king will answer them, "Truly I tell you, just as you did it to one of the least of these who are my brethren you did it to me."

Mark 8:18   *Having eyes do you not see, and having ears do you not hear?*

Mark 9:33-35 And when they came to Capernaum and when he was in the house he asked them, "What were you discussing on the way?" But they were silent, for on the way they had discussed with one another who was the greatest. And he sat down and called the twelve; and he said to them, "If any of you would be first he must be last of all and the servant of all."

Mark 12:30 You shall love the Lord your God with all you heart, and with all your soul, and with all your mind, and with all your strength.

Mark 12:34   And when Jesus saw that he answered wisely he said to him, "You are not far from the Kingdom of God."

Luke 17:20-21 Once Jesus was asked by the Pharisees when the Kingdom of God was coming, and he answered, "The Kingdom of God is not coming with things that can be observed; nor will they say, 'Look, here it is!' or 'There it is!' For in fact the Kingdom of God is among you." (or "within you").

John 8: 31-32   Then Jesus said to the Jews who had believed in him, "If you continue in my word then you are my disciples indeed, and you shall come to know the truth and the truth shall make you free."

Romans 7:19 For I do not do the good that I want, but the evil that I do not want is what I do.

Romans 7:24-25 Wretched person that I am. Who will rescue me from this body of death? Thanks be to God through Jesus Christ our Lord.

II Corinthians 5:19: In Christ God was reconciling the world to himself, not counting their trespasses against them, and entrusting to us the message of reconciliation.

Philippians 4:13 I can do all things through the one who empowers me.

7. A Better Way to Go

One of the ladies of the congregation dropped by my office to talk with me about Ellen Glynston. I appreciated her directness. Usually visitors chatted on about nothing in particular until they felt comfortable enough to bring up the reason for their visit. I had grown to accept this process, and even enjoyed the banter. Still I wished they would cut to the chase. I was a student minister trying to balance ministerial duties, studies and family. There never seemed to be enough time to handle all the important details of life. Idle chatter was low on my priority list. It took me a moment to recall who Ellen was. I mentally ranged over the pews, checking the faces of the those filling them. Almost all had their customary places. Then my mind spotted her - a quiet, gray-haired lady seated in the back right section. She rarely spoke, but was always well-dressed, well-mannered. My visitor told me that Ellen had cancer and was taking radiation treatments at Foote Hospital in Jackson. The reason for the visit was that Ellen needed someone to drive her to the hospital on Thursdays. Would I do it? Of course I would. It would be no trouble for me. I would use the time driving and waiting to work out my sermon or organize one of my term papers. I calculated that it would require about a half hour to drive each way, and the treatment would consume another half hour. I would allot an hour and a half each Thursday morning.

I arrived at Ellen's house on Thursday morning. She was waiting for me, and came out as I drove up. We exchanged greetings as she got into the car, and we drove to Jackson in silence. I assumed she was lost in her own thoughts, as I was in mine. I read in the parking lot while she underwent her radiation therapy. She returned with a shy smile. I

74

asked her how she felt. She assured me she was fine, and we drove home in relative silence.

We repeated this basic theme for the next two weeks. I drove to her house. She came to the car. We exchanged pleasantries. We drove in silence, she lost in her thoughts, and I mentally writing some paper or sermon. I was doing my job. She seemed happy with the arrangement. The church members who knew of this were pleased. It was no bother, really.

The next week, when she returned to the parking lot after her treatment, she seated herself in the car, turned to me, and shying inquired, "May I show you a better way to go?" I assumed she wanted to take a different route than the major highway. This would take more time, of course, but she was a nice person, so I agreed. Ellen led me through the back roads, winding through Michigan Center, along the Chain-of-Lakes. I had heard of them, but in my two years at Napoleon I had never taken the time to see them. I learned what I had missed. They were lovely.

The narrow, winding roads required that I drive slowly, so I had the opportunity to actually see and enjoy the scenery. There were a series of small lakes, surrounded by shady trees and small cottages. A few boats moved leisurely across them, making tiny ripples as they parted the surface. A few sat motionless while fishermen idly cast their lures into waiting waters. Some children played in the water off their docks while their parents watched. Now and then I noticed someone cooking lunch over an outdoor grill.

Ellen began to talk as we drove. She told me of her growing up days in the area, and how she enjoyed the lakes in every season. I pictured these lakes frozen by the winter's chill - with ice fishing shanties scattered about, young skaters speeding their way, and older ones holding hands as they glided along together. I shared some of my remembrances from lakes and waters. The return trip undoubtedly took longer than usual, but I simply did not notice it. When we finally arrived at Ellen's house, she got out and thanked me as she usually did . . . but this time I believed I noticed a sly smile of satisfaction on her face as she departed.

That smile caused me to reflect upon what had happened. "May I show you a better to way to go?" she had inquired. I had to wonder if she meant only the winding path through the Chain-of-Lakes, or if she had been pointing me in another - far more important direction. Whichever it was, the time had been well spent, and I really was no farther behind in my work than if I had taken the highway home.

Ellen had gently set my foot upon the path of another portion of my journey.

I would like to say that I had some immediate understanding of this, and that my life instantly took on a softer, more serene color. But Carl Jung was correct when he likened the soul to the agricultural dimension of our being. He said that although the mind might quickly grasp some truth it took time for the soul to change, heal, and grow. By the time I had heard that truism I had added enough experience to recognize its truth, and could appreciate more fully Jesus' many attempts to liken the Kingdom of God to the agricultural aspect of life. In between time I was to speed along many highways, race across many fields . . . and charge down many a blind alley before I grasped the simple truth Ellen had given me that long-ago morning.

At Adrian College, where I was completing my undergraduate degree, I taught Freshman English on a fellowship, while carrying a full academic load. I also sang the lead role in a musical, played solo clarinet in the band, and was on the debate team. When nominated for "Who's Who on Campus" I laughingly declined, suggesting that I actually should be up for "Who's He on Campus." I was recognized by many, but actually known by - and knew - very few.

At seminary, while others chatted over breakfast, lunch and dinner, I often chose to sit alone going over my Greek vocabulary cards. Seminary was my one chance to garner all the tools I could find which would aid me in my ministry. Time was too important to waste over idle chit chat. Although I enjoyed the convenience of the new, main dormitory I moved to the third floor of an older one where there were fewer "drop-ins" to interrupt my studies.

I took a brief hiatus from my doctoral studies and accepted an assignment to organize a new congregation in the emerging northeast side of Ann Arbor, Michigan near the new North Campus. The opportunity was too tempting to decline. Although this took every moment I had available I still spent time maintaining my studies and doing whatever reading I could to keep an awareness of current events. This, too, was important for a preacher in an academic community.

One evening I was lost in my newspaper when one of my young daughters decided she needed some of my attention. What followed looked like a scene from the theater of the absurd. She tried to snuggle up to me and for reasons quite unknown to me at the time I decided to resist. After all, this was *my* private time. I needed it. I merely moved the paper into the space she was trying to occupy. She arose and tried to approach me from the other direction. I, in turn, crossed my legs in that direction and repositioned the paper. This sparring went on for a few minutes during which my sense of annoyance was increasing. It was now a battle of wills. I was the father. She was the child. I was the one in charge. It was that simple. Then she took another approach. She moved between my legs stuck her head under the paper and crawled up - with outstretched arms - and a gorgeous, inviting smile. My earlier resolve faded into nothingness I dropped the paper and scooped her up into my arms, hugged her, and kissed her . . . and she shyly asked, "Aren't you glad I'm persistent?" The words of Scripture echoed somewhere in my soul: ". . . and a little child shall lead them ." (Isaiah 11:6) It was a powerful lesson, but only one of many my soul still needed to learn.

A few years later I preached a sermon based upon Matthew 7:12, *Whatever you would have people do to you, do likewise to them.* I preached it as a reaction to the putdown humor being popularized by some ill-mannered comedians. I entitled it, "Let's Play Pickup." At the conclusion I called for the members of the congregation to give affirmation to at least two other people before they departed, and to continue to give at least one affirmation per day for the remainder of the week. When the service was over, I stepped to one side to watch "my people" give and receive affirmations. To my amazement a few walked over to me, hugged me, and told me they loved me.

I melted! Right on the spot. I retained my composure, and replied to the effect that I loved them, as well . . . but I melted . . . deep down inside, the warmth of that expressed love melted some barrier within me of which I was totally unaware. Diane and my daughters loved me. I knew that. They were family. Family loved family. That was a given. I had never had anyone outside the family tell me that I was loved by them. The thought was foreign to me. I suppose that if I had thought of it at all I would have wondered how anyone - that is *anyone who really knew me could love me.* This was to start me on a focused journey which wrapped these earlier incidents into an understandable package. It was a journey which - once begun - could never end. It was a journey which really is a "better way to go."

There was some portion of me which, again, felt like John Wesley, the founding father of Methodism, who confessed that he who had come to America to bring salvation to the natives realized that he, himself, was in need of salvation. My understanding of salvation was expressed in an entirely different manner from John's however. I had little concern as to the location of my eternal resting place . Rather, I was searching to fill the empty spaces, tear down the inner barriers to intimacy, and heal the wounds within my soul.

This particular pilgrimage, like every inner quest, had to go back to its beginnings. My early childhood days were filled with adventures. My father owned a boat and sporting goods business. This overflowed into a host of exciting activities. Dad owned a midget racing car, and we went to the track regularly to watch it run. We were even allowed to go into the pit area and talk with the drivers. We also owned (or technically "sponsored") various outboard racing boats, and spent many a summer's day at the lakes watching them compete. We were taught rifle marksmanship, archery, bowling, boxing, and skeet shooting. At one time my brother, George, and I had the two fastest miniature racing cars in the state, and we regularly participated in meets and tournaments. Dad also was a member of a fine magic club. There was always a new magician who would teach us tricks by which we could amaze and amuse our friends. On Sunday evenings, we would dine out at one of the many restaurants where my father was known by the owner or head waiter. In some of the restaurants we skipped the menu, went into the kitchen, and ordered from the chef. However, if nothing special was happening on a Sunday, my father would read the papers and take a nap after the noon meal. Then he would tell us he had to go the office to take care of some work.

I did not realize it at the time but my father was what is termed a "workaholic." It probably was the work of Ann Wilson Schaef which caused me to recognize this and to realize how that addiction to busyness of my father's affected me.1 Ann observed that the purpose of all addictions is to avoid intimacy. It's an unconscious purpose, to be sure. Most people would tell you they seek genuine intimacy, and they probably believe that to be true. However, I have come to realize that most of us are also afraid of genuine intimacy. It makes us vulnerable. Further, before we are genuinely able to be intimate with another person we must first become intimate with ourselves. This means taking off our masks and seeing ourselves for who we really are. It means standing naked before the mirror of our souls - without sucking in our spiritual stomach.

It's more than most of us wish to do. And that, I believe, is precisely why Jesus said the road is narrow and few will discover it (Matthew 7:14).

The safest place to begin, of course, was in analyzing my father's illness. Dad was one of those persons to whom most people were instantly attracted. He had charisma. He was one of the best story tellers I ever heard. He could entertain people for hours, leaving everyone with the belief that they knew him and he was their friend. This belief in their friendship was well-founded. My father was generous to a fault with anyone he knew. He would give of whatever was needed to help a friend in distress. He just had no idea how to give of his inner self, either to himself or to another person. So he filled his hours with activities. His mind was always on something outside of himself, so that neither he nor anyone else knew who that self was. He died far too early at age sixty-five. At his funeral, a crony of his, a crusty inspector of homicide, told me that the week before he died my father looked at him with a previously unseen sense of openness and said, "I am so terribly lonely." The inspector had not known how to respond, so the invitation went unanswered.

The next safest step was to observe how other people use busyness to avoid intimacy. This was easy and obvious once you cued into the idea. I noted that John Wesley was addicted to busyness. John kept himself and all his clergy as busy as possible "doing the Lord's work." I also noted that he never was able to have a decent relationship with a woman. John veritably worshipped busyness. It still is the secret to being a successful minister. As a practical matter it appears to be the key to being "successful" in most endeavors. The one who puts in the overtime gets the promotion - gets the money - gets the job security.

The more difficult and demanding step was the self-examination - the standing naked before God and self. This can only be done if you really believe the Good News of Jesus that God forgives all your failings. If we can understand God as a loving parent - not a wrathful judge - who wants our redemption, not our punishment, then we may find the courage to remove the masks we wear, even in secret, and see just who we really are. Paul says it so well in I Corinthians 13:12, "*Now we see in a mirror dimly, but then face to face. Now I know in part; then I shall understand fully, even as I have been fully understood.*" The key to all this, says Paul is God's agape love. Once we understand it and accept it we are able to muster the courage to look clearly into that mirror and see what God has seen all along.

I cannot relate the entirety of this exploration of my naked soul. One reason is that it is nowhere near completion. Another is that it is far too personal. I keep meeting myself coming around corners. Just when I think I have acquired an understanding of some facet of my personhood I encounter quite another dimension. I marvel that such complexity can be contained in so small a space, and I tremble as I recall the words spoken by the Geresene demonic when asked by Jesus to tell him his name: "*My name is Legion for we are many.*" (Mark 5:9) As I prowl through the labyrinth of my soul I continually encounter persons I have been and in some sense still am. They are a collection of frightened, shy, curious, sensual, playful, obedient children; and cocky, confused, boisterous, aggressive teenagers. I recognize the boy scout who teems with patriotism, loyalty, and integrity. But I also recognize his counterpart lurking somewhere in the shadows. I see the bright scholar and the inept handyman, the courageous warrior and the coward. I see the idealist side by side with the schemer. I have come to appreciate ever more the confusion of Paul who wondered why he was forever failing to do all the good a portion of him desired to do, while inevitably doing far more of those things his better nature told him were unworthy. (Romans 7:19)

I realize that it was far easier to wrestle with theology than to wrestle with God. It is more comfortable to grapple with ideas of God, particularly when you have been academically equipped to do so, than to encounter God in the commonplace of daily living, in the struggles, the temptations, the failures, the feelings of inadequacies, the moments of tiny victories . . . the give and take of relationships which long to be more than they are, but fear to become too precious as well. To back track a bit, I now understand more fully why I wrapped myself in my work rather than engaging other people where they were. Partly it was a habit derived from my family of origin. I was merely following the pattern established by my father (perhaps something of the sins [failures] of the parents are in fact visited to the children of the third and fourth generation). I actually had no idea that relationships could run deeper than those I had experienced - just as someone who has never experienced music, smelled the scent of a flower, or seen a magnificent sunrise could conceive of such wonders.

It is more comfortable to relate on the surface, each player maintaining his or her mask and role . . agreeing not to peer too closely at the others. We keep our minds occupied with trivia in order to avoid dealing with truth. We chit chat about weather, sports, politics, and everything else but what matters, and what we could actually act upon if we were to be confronted with it. We immerse ourselves in our work or hobbies. We lose ourselves in reading or television. We spend time *along side* of one another and are rarely really *with* another person. This fills our time, and gives us a false sense of connectedness.

I believe our busyness addiction sometimes stems from our reluctance to peer too deeply into our own souls for fear of stumbling across some of the painful memories that dwell therein. No one makes it through childhood intact - without a few scars or embarrassing moments best left lurking in the shadows. I still flinch inwardly when I recall the

81

humiliation I felt at every spelling bee. Because of my speech defect I had chosen to play ignorant rather than face the awkwardness of having the teacher ask me what letter I was attempting to pronounce, and listening to the giggles that murmured through the class as a result. Few of us are so perfect that there was not some defect (perhaps exaggerated in our mind) which served as a target for some of the sharp tongued in our class or neighborhood. Few of us have not had the painful or awkward moments which we would rather leave hidden in the trash pile of our souls. We may also harbor feelings and dreams which we would not want those who are important to us to know.

I have been most blessed by an abundance of friends. Many of these friends were close, warm and supportive guides along life's path. Still, there always was a point beyond which even the closest friends could not pass. It may be that I would not, or could not, invite them to come closer. Perhaps it was simply that they refused the invitation for reasons of their own. It was at that point of impasse where I experienced being alone. To one extent or another I believe this is the common experience of us all. There are lonely places in our souls which hunger to be shared, to be understood . . . to be accepted and loved.

Years ago, while still a teenager I experienced this vague, gnawing hunger while surrounded by people in a busy area in Detroit. It prompted me to write this verse:

> The city clang, clang, clangs all day,
> And its people rush to and fro and forth and farther on,
> Never knowing or caring for those they meet on their way,
> As they come and go and pass by and are gone.
> And I come and go and stand there,
> Unknown to each as each is strange to me.
> The loneliness seems more than I can bear.
> Strange, that in a forest one should want a tree.

Years later I read the account in Mark of Jesus attempting to restore the sight of a man. After placing his hands on the man's eyes, he asked him what he saw. The man replied, "I see people, but they look like trees walking." (Mark 8:24). Mark then reports that Jesus touched the man a second time, and this time he could see all things clearly. I remember thinking that this malady extends beyond those who are visually impaired. Perhaps, I thought, we all need a second touch.

Salvation by faith means far more than mere intellectual assent to theological propositions. *Faith* as used by the early Christians called for participation in the object of that trust. I believe this is what Paul meant when he wrote, *"If anyone is in Christ he is a new creation. ; the old has passed away, behold, the new has come. (II Corinthians 5:17).* Later he elaborated on this: *"Examine yourselves to see whether you are holding to your faith. Test yourselves. Do you not realize that Christ is in you? - unless indeed you fail to meet the test!" (II Corinthians 13:5)* So many well-intentioned Christians have a strong belief *about* Jesus Christ. However they do not grasp the concept of being *in* Christ. We learn *about* Jesus Christ from Scripture and teachers. However, according to Paul, we *encounter* Jesus Christ within ourselves.

If we are to move beyond the barriers which separate us we need to find a better way than the one we have been traveling. Somewhere in the midst of overly-crowded calendars we can locate a time - and times - for nurturing our own souls. Sometime in that calendar we can find moments for inscaping our souls with beauty, for pausing to experience the moment in which we find ourselves . . . with the people who are present to us. Sometime in that busy calendar we can schedule moments in which we may delve beneath the masks we wear, and rest in the silence of eternity with the One who is eternal, who knows us far better than we can ever know ourselves . . . and still loves us all the same. There in the calmness of inner space those broken, frightened portions of our souls can be known, loved, touched and healed.

Any journey toward intimacy must begin from within. That is my next lesson. The next button to refasten correctly. The next step taken along life's spiritual path.

1Ann Wilson Schaef *When Society Becomes an Addict, Harper & Row, 1986.*

REFLECTIONS

According to Carol S. Pearson, in her book, *Awakening the Heroes Within*, two archetypes which need to work together in some harmonious relationship are The Seeker and The Lover. If one pursues the Seeker apart from the drive and power of the Lover, one becomes the lonely hunter. If we are totally goal oriented we tend to neglect people along the way. That is easy to do, particularly for those of us who tend to avoid revealing too much of ourselves in an intimate relationship. It was my awakening to being loved which helped me on my journey. We may have difficulty accepting the fact that people might love us in spite of - and because of - who we are. When we peek beneath the surface and view ourselves we rarely, if ever, measure up to what we have set as an acceptable standard. Consequently we fear that if anyone ever really knew us they would reject us. Our distorted understanding of the Christian faith often is at fault here. We tend to think more in terms of judgment than grace, of retribution rather than redemption. We, ourselves, become the judge of ourselves, just as we become the judge of others. We cannot escape it. Once we fall into the judgmental mode, we are stuck in it . . . to the detriment of our own spiritual well-being.

QUESTIONS FOR REFLECTION AND DISCUSSION

1. What are your busyness addictions that keep you from closer interaction with family and friends?

2. What shadows, wounds, or scars do you carry from childhood that interfere with your personal relationships?

3. Who is your closest (most intimate) friend? If you placed that person on an intimacy scale ranging from 1 to 100 what would the score be?

4. Are there parts of yourself you hide from? If yes, why?

5. Have you tried giving those parts to God-in-Christ, to find release and redemption?

SCRIPTURE REFERENCES

Matthew 7:12   Whatever you would have people do to you, do likewise to them.

Matthew 7:14 But small is the gate and narrow the road that leads to life, and very few find it.

Mark 5:9   My name is Legion for we are many.

Mark 8:24 I see people, but they look like trees walking.

Romans 7:19   For I do not do the good I want, but the evil I do not want is what I do.

I Corinthians 13:12, Now we see in a mirror dimly, but then face to face. Now I know in part; then I shall understand fully, even as I have been fully understood.

II Corinthians 5:17   If anyone is in Christ he is a new creation; the old has passed away, behold, the new has come.

II Corinthians 13:5   Examine yourselves to see whether you are holding to your faith. Test yourselves. Do you not realize that Christ is in you? - unless indeed you fail to meet the test!

Isaiah 11:6b . . . and a little child shall lead them.

8. LOST AND FOUND

In the daily struggle for survival and success it is easy to become so caught up in the physical world that we become oblivious to the spiritual. Yet it is the spiritual which underlies the physical, giving meaning and purpose to all that is and all that we do. If we even pause to consider our origins we must realize that the spiritual dimension preceded the physical. Before there was time and space and matter and movement there was that which gave rise to it all. There was God. Genesis 1:1 says it simply but probably not at all in the manner we understand it today: "*In the beginning God . . ..*" The scientists may call it the Big Bang but it remains for the religionist, the spiritually-minded, to ask who and why? Paul expressed it well in Acts 17:28: "*For in him we live and move and have our being.*"

I must admit that this dimension escaped me in the early days of my ministry. I know I read Paul's statement but it went right past my consciousness. Somewhere in my studies of church history I encountered the great mystics of the faith: Meister Eckhart, Juliana of Norwich, Thomas á Kempis, and Teresa of Avila. At the time I did not pay much heed to them. I considered them apart from the mainstream of the church; quaint, but not practical. I was stuck somewhere in the belief that one became a Christian and then earned entrance into heaven by a combination of faith and good works.

As I reflect upon my seminary days, I realize that I somehow missed the spiritual dimension of our faith. It might have been my focus upon the academics. It may have been a reflection of the times. Spirituality was not in vogue in the 60's. Society was focused upon civil rights, Viet Nam, and the new sexual freedom. As I picked up the specialized vocabulary of my faith I equated *spiritual* with *emotional*. I gave it lip service, but had little or no understanding of what it meant in practical terms. I prayed, both publicly and privately, but this was the extent of my spiritual pursuit. Or so I thought at the time.

Just as I had experienced a vague hunger for a deeper personal intimacy, I came to realize that I also harbored a subterranean hunger for a sense of the divine in my life - for a deeper spirituality. Our new congregation in Ann Arbor was growing, and doing exciting things. Yet, no accomplishment generated a lasting satisfaction. Some portion of my life felt like a car racing down a freeway, trying to get somewhere other than where I was, believing life could be better just a bit farther down the road. I kept setting goals, meeting them, then setting new ones, assuming I would eventually attain one that would allow me to relax. Yet, there was a void within me that could not be filled by activities or attainments. I was oblivious to that fact, though. I was young, full of energy and ambition. Life was exciting and teeming with possibilities. I was involved in bringing in the Kingdom, surrounded by a host of the faithful, exceptionally talented, and energetic friends. We were making an impact on society. We were fulfilling our callings as Christians.

I was running on empty, and did not know it.

I was trying to do everything on my own, and it was taking a toll. In this regard I was not alone. I believe this is the malady that drives much of America. In spite of our claims of faith and trust in God, we rely on ourselves - and ourselves alone - to provide the strength and understanding to make our lives work as *we* believe they should. As a result we jump start ourselves with caffeine, drive too fast while playing our radios or chatting on our cellular phones to keep from feeling alone. We work too much , then race home and eat too much and drink too much . . . and sleep too little, so that we do not have to lie in bed with nothing to distract us from our own thoughts.

Then all heaven broke loose! It was Pentecost all over again in little Ann Arbor. The Word of God Community erupted almost overnight in a Roman Catholic campus church. The people claimed to have experienced the Holy Spirit powerfully in their lives, and they were *excited*! They invited their friends and neighbors to their meetings. Before long almost every congregation in the city had some of its members attending their Sunday evening services. At first I thought it was a novelty. Then I began to see some of the results. A young campus couple began attending my services. They were dressed in the fashion of the Ann Arbor 70's. Both looked as though they had found their clothes in a back alley. His hair was shoulder length. Their footwear might generously be described as sandals. I had become accustomed to this garb, and might not have noticed it except that, after attending for about a month, they made an appointment to talk with me. At our meeting the young man told me he had been "busted" for smoking pot a few months earlier and was out on bail. He had roamed into a Word of God service, and had experienced the Spirit in his life. Now he wanted to get his life in order. He planned to plead guilty to the drug charge, because he *was* guilty and wanted to settle that properly. Then he and his girl who had been living together for some time planned to marry and set that portion of their life in order, as well. They both seemed sincere in their motives. There was no attempt to get me to intervene with the local authorities. They simply needed to be honest with me as they became part of my congregation. It was essential to their new life in Christ. Then they thanked me and went about getting their lives in order.

I should have thanked *them*. They had reminded me of what I had lost in my life, and pointed me toward where I might find it again.

This spirit thing had to be taken seriously. It was shortly after this that I met with my seminary doctoral committee to discuss my dissertation which dealt with patristic Trinitarian issues. At the meeting one of my professors asked me about the Word of God Community. His attitude was condescending - much like mine was earlier. My response was that some of their adherents stopped using drugs and changed their lives (I knew of a few others by then). I added, that in so far as I knew no one from my congregation or any of the other United Methodist congregations in the town had stopped using drugs as a result of our services. He looked surprised, as frankly I was surprised to hear myself admitting that, and the subject was changed.

Now I turned once more to those quaint mystics I had briefly read about at seminary. Most of my library was academically-oriented, but one of Diane's books, published by the Upper Room as a devotional aid, seemed to jump up and say, "read me." It was *Moments with the Devotional Masters.*1 It had been laying around the house for years, but I had never noticed it. Now that I was ready to read it seriously, it seemed to appear. I recalled a proverb that says, "When the student is ready, the teacher appears." As I read the quotes from these early church mystics I saw a pattern in their thinking:

There is only one road that leads to God, and that is prayer. If anyone shows you another you are being deceived. Teresa of Avila.

It is His good pleasure to reign in our understanding, and sit in our soul restfully, and to dwell in our soul endlessly. Juliana of Norwich.

I am as sure as that I live that nothing is so near to me as God. Meister Eckhart.

The goods of God which are beyond all measure can only be contained in an empty and solitary heart. John of the Cross.

All of these quiet heroes of the faith were asserting the certainty of God in their lives. There had been a time when I could have echoed their words. I had been working on the assumption that because I was doing the Lord's work we were in some kind of partnership. We were working side by side; hand in hand. This was not necessarily true, though. I was not acting like a partner. I was operating more like someone who has been given a franchise. I could see that my prayer life had become perfunctory. It was one of those things I did as a pastor. "Dick, would you ask the blessing?" or "Would you offer a prayer for us?" I prayed on request and at worship services. Prior to entering the ministry and in my early days at Napoleon, my prayer life was as natural as conversation with a close friend. Somewhere along the line I had allowed my personal prayer life to deteriorate into a morning habit, like brushing my teeth.

With this realization I decided to spend time reminiscing. It was like those occasions when we are searching the attic or garage for some item and happen to stumble across an old photo album or year book. We pause and browse through it to recall what we were like in those earlier days. We may notice the difference in girth and wonder how we let our appetite and love of ease cause us to neglect our body. The difference here was that I saw I had focused so completely into my mind and the intellectual dimension of our faith that I had neglected my soul. As I reflected upon this I recalled an anecdote I had heard long before the days of automobile seat belts. As a comfortably married couple were driving along the road the wife coyly mentioned to her husband that they used to sit much closer together when they were courting. His response, as he looked at her seated by her window was, "I'm not the one who moved." If God was absent from my life, it was not that God had abandoned me. I was the one who had moved.

I do not recall who said it, but when I first heard it I recognized that it was true: The last great frontier is not outer space, but *inner* space. It obviously was my time to begin the exploration.

There is a difference between the *Spirit* of God and the *Presence* of God. The books of The Old Testament often speak of the presence of God. God was present with Adam, (Genesis 3:8) with Cain (Genesis 4:16), with Moses (Exodus 3:5-6), with Joshua and the children of Israel (Joshua 6:27), and with Hannah and Samuel (I Samuel 2:21). By New Testament times the Greek concept of God as totally transcendent had rendered the possibility of our experiencing God's Presence inconceivable. Instead, there was the frequent use of the term *Spirit*. Even so, the Spirit is experienced within the individual whereas the Presence is felt as being exterior.

Many of you have had the experience of sensing an unseen presence. There was no sound, but you were aware of a presence nonetheless. When you checked it out you found there was another entity *present* with you. It may have been a person or it may have been an animal. There have also been occasions when you sensed a presence, and turned to see someone staring at you. In that respect the person staring was *present* to you, and you sensed that. Some people are a bit more sensitive

90

to a presence than the average person. However, the fact remains that there was a presence, and you experienced it, or someone was *present to you* and you sensed that.

I had a most unusual - but memorable experience of that one evening. At my first church, the congregation had decided to modernize my office. It still resembled the kitchen it once had been, and they decided it was time to make it more presentable and useable. Temporarily it resembled a workshop complete with building materials strewn everywhere. I was at work on a sermon, using the quiet of the evening as a means of focusing my thoughts. Then I sensed a strong awareness of another presence.   There was no one in the room, so I called out to the emptiness of the building: "Who's there?" Silence was the only response, so I returned to my work. Still, the sense of another presence crept back into my consciousness, so I called out again, and received the same nothingness of a response. This repeated itself a few more times until I found it impossible to focus on my work. I stood up and began to follow this sense of presence to where it might lead. If someone had looked in on me they might have thought I had taken leave of my senses. I was prowling around the room like one of those water diviners, hands raised to chest level. I only lacked the tree branch to make the picture complete. Finally I was drawn to a stack of tiles, covered with an empty, upside down box. I slowly lifted the box and spied a tiny mouse - - - peacefully asleep. "I knew you were here someplace," I thought, as I replaced his cover and gently removed him from the building.

So what does this have to do with the point I am making? A great deal! I *knew* there was another presence with me in that room. I was as certain of it as if I had actually experienced it with one of my five physical senses.   In a similar manner I *know* I have sensed the presence of the Divine in my life at various times . . . as have many of you.

My first experience of the Divine came shortly after I became a Christian at age twenty-three. I had been assigned to the Artillery School at Ft. Sill, Oklahoma. There I had attended the Lawton Heights Methodist Church and had been strongly moved by their minister, the Rev. R.C. Veirs. Suddenly, the Christian faith made sense to me, and I longed to be a part of it. I kept waiting for some powerful experience. I hung around the church and spent time near the altar railing, figuring that is where "IT" might happen. One night as I sat in the living room of our house as Diane was preparing dinner, I felt Him . . . as surely as I have ever felt the presence of anyone. I was enveloped by a sense of peace and security. No words were exchanged but I knew - I *knew* - no matter what might happen in the near future, everything was as it should be . . . everything would be okay.

I started a practice of regular evening prayer, although I had thought of this as conversation at the time . . . nothing formal .. . no folded hands or bended knee. Yet, this time was vitally important. It was a way of putting the day to rest, of sorting through the many events to see what had been worthwhile and what had not, to understand how I might have made things better, and to figure out why I had acted as I did. One evening as I was driving home as part of what a local disk jockey dubbed "The Bumper-to-Bumper Club" I became aware of a song writing itself in my head:

I talk with my Father in the evening
As I stand at the end of a day.
I ask him to forgive the way I sometimes live:
The things I do and say.

I talk with my Father in the evening,
And I open my soul to His ears.
I tell him of my dreams, my problems, my schemes
And I know that my Father always hears.

He speaks to me in quiet tones of truth and love so grand.
I feel a joy I've never known as we stand hand in hand.

I talk with my Father in the evening,
And believe the things He has to say.
When He tells me of the love and joy above,
And I know I'll be with Him there some day.

As I heard the words in my head I knew they expressed my feelings about those "after-hour chats." Those moments had been so good, so worthy, and yet so peaceful. I do not know why I stopped them, but I had. And just as an absence of exercise - or proper nutrients - eventually makes itself known to the body, so this absence of the divine Presence in my life was now revealing itself in my soul. I might still be quoting Philippians 4:13 *"I can do all things through the one who empowers me."* but I had gradually closed myself off from that power. Instead of being focused, my life was losing itself in diversions.

The story we call the Prodigal Son came to mind. My real episode of being the prodigal had taken place back in my late teens. I had let intellectual arrogance, coupled with wanderlust lead me into a time of practical atheism. That had ended when I met Diane and began to rebuild my religious life as part of our growing relationship. Still, there was some portion of me that related to that long-ago prodigal. What had happened was not an intentional abandonment of the faith. Rather it was a casual redirection of priorities that had caused me to stray away. This realization caused me to wince inside. I know that the Greek word *planeo* means "I stray." The term planet describes those heavenly bodies that stray through the evening sky rather than following the ordered movement of the other stars. *Planeo* is often translated as "I sin." I could understand that this sin-of-straying-away was probably the more common form of sinning - of falling short or missing the mark. We simply become so involved in secular - or even religious - affairs that our personal prayer life falls into disrepair ... without our even realizing it. Since this realization I have observed a multitude of clergy and active laity who at least *appear* to pray more for the effect on the listeners than as an act of real communication with God. It is a trap awaiting us all. The real purpose of these intimate encounters should not be to tell God what we want, but to discern God's will for our life.

Through the years, my prayer life has changed, grown and matured. I have found that prayer serves a multitude of purposes, and it is best not to confuse them or try to lump them all together. All prayer for me must begin with a time of silent centering. I simply cannot close my eyes and start praying words, or it simply becomes chatter. Diane and I have learned not to come into the house when we have been absent for a time, and start chattering at the other person. First we need to present ourselves to the other, perhaps we simply hug - or place ourselves before the other as a presence. Then we can speak and it does not require as many words.

Touch me before you speak.
I need to close the distance between you and me,
I need to sense you as a presence in my life,
And to feel you as a presence in mine.
Touch me, then we can speak, and the words can be few.
Touch me, then we can speak and know that we both understand
. . . and we both are understood.

I spend the first few minutes of prayer in quiet meditation. If seated in a chair my back is straight but relaxed. If seated on a cushion, I cross my legs gently. I let whatever thoughts enter my head fly by and dissolve in the silence. I do not focus on them. I concentrate gently on my breathing, feeling myself sink slowly beneath the surface of my being and into the depths. I usually arrive at a point where - even with closed eyes - I sense a brightness. I would like to say that I always sense His Presence, but I do not. Rather I know from experience that He is always near, and I sense myself in His Presence.

Sometimes the entire focus of the prayer is intercessory. There are those for whose needs I pray. The first time I ever attempted this was when I volunteered to be part of a continuing prayer chain. The hour I selected was three in the morning, and I was to pray for an hour for people who were at a retreat. Frankly I wondered how I could ever remain in prayer for an entire hour. I looked at the list, and jumped in. Somewhere along the way I delved into their inner lives, realizing that they, like I, struggled with duality, were filled with contradictions, probably were grasping for stars beyond their reach, bore deep concern for others as well as for themselves, and undoubtedly were trying to make sense of the many roles they were called upon to play on life's broad stage. I began to pray for these inner struggles of these spiritual pilgrims. In praying for them I was, in some way, praying for myself since we possess more similarities than we might care to admit. When I eventually paused to see how much longer I was "on prayer duty" I saw I had gone well beyond the scheduled time. I had *lost* myself in prayer . . . and it felt good. I had been immersed in humankind.

I cannot say precisely how intercessory prayer works. I also do not understand exactly what causes a light bulb to light up when I flip a wall switch. I do know, however, that I have come to trust in both processes. This is not to say that everything I pray for automatically happens. Every prayer is not answered as I wish. Still, I believe every prayer is answered. There must always be the *"Yet, not what I want, but what you want,"* which Jesus prayed in Gethsemane (Mark 14: 36b) I do believe our prayers serve as an instrument for God's grace, and some good things happen which would not happen had there not been prayers. Sometimes the results are almost startling. Recently, at a healing service, I was approached by a young couple. The wife suffered from hives. She had been to numerous specialists without receiving relief. Her desperation had caused her to come forward for healing prayers. I anointed her with oil, lay my hands on her and offered a prayer. About ten days later, at a church dinner, she approached me to tell me her hives had begun to clear up the next morning, and were completely gone within two days. My only response was that her faith had made her whole. I was delighted but not surprised. This sort of thing has occurred many times. As I said, I do not understand it, but I have come to trust in the process.

One Wednesday evening, just before I was to speak at a church prayer service I was told of a young member of the congregation who was in the hospital with a diagnosis of viral meningitis. He was in ICU and doctors did not know whether or not he would live through the night. I used the model from Mark of the friends who lowered their paralyzed companion through a roof to bring him to Jesus (Mark 2:1-12). In a directed meditation I asked everyone to collectively bring the young man before Jesus and lift him up for healing . . . and to hold him there throughout the evening. The young man went home two days later. He was completely healed. He had no idea that we were praying for him until much later. Coincidence? Misdiagnosis? Lucky break?

As I said, I have come to trust in the process.

The primary purpose of intercessory prayer is to act as conduits for God's grace. A side effect seems to be that in doing so we dissolve our own ego-centricity in our concern for others. More importantly, I believe any form of prayer immerses us in the spiritual dimension of life, and draws us ever closer to God and God's power.

Sometimes I am content merely to remain in the meditative state, without silently verbalizing any concern. It is somewhat like sitting in a room with some very fond friend. You do not need to share words. It is enough to sense the other's presence, to bask in the warmth of the relationship, and to feel joy in the remembrance of things shared.

One form of prayer which I find very rewarding follows this pattern: I close my eyes, center my body, then mentally walk to some quiet place. A favorite place is the hillside in Galilee near where they claim the Sermon on the Mount was preached. You can see the roof tops of Capernaum, and I rather imagine it is the place where Jesus went on occasion for his prayer time. I walk down the road to where there are boulders, heaved to the surface by some earlier quake. It is just past a citrus grove and I can smell the rich fragrance as I approach the rocks. Seated on one is the One I seek. His eyes are closed in prayer. I place myself on a rock next to him and wait silently. The sea of Galilee sparkles below in the sunlight. Perhaps a sailboat glides slowly along the shore. As I wait, I gather my thoughts and center my soul. Eventually, I sense He is present for me. Then I pour out whatever is in my heart, knowing He will understand and still accept me. At some point I sense the moment should be ended. He nods, raises his hand in an untouched blessing, and I depart. These moments may last from five minutes to fifteen or more. Each time I return to the present moment feeling quieted, loved, and gently blessed.

A daily ritual is the self-exploratory prayer. This is the evening conversation with God in which I go over the events of the day, celebrating the victories and good moments, and giving thanks for the gift of that day. Then together we look at the events that did not work out as desired, and the trouble spots where there was conflict. Whenever I attempt to place the responsibility on others I hear His voice asking, "What could you have done differently, Dick?" There is no blame in his tone. There is only the open-ended question. However, the words of I John 1: 8-10 always seem to lie just beneath the surface: *"If we claim to be without sin (failings), we deceive ourselves and the truth is not in us.*

96

If we confess our sins, he is faithful and just and will forgive us our sins and purify us from all unrighteousness. If we claim we have not sinned, we make him out to be a liar, and his word has no place in our lives." I also have to remember that if I claim it is other people who are responsible for my difficulties and failures I am reducing myself to being a victim and am without power to change. But I [really] can do all things through the One who empowers me. (Philippians 4:13), and I cannot change the actions of other people. I must change my own actions and reactions.

It would be nice to say that this causes some immediate inner change, and that I instantly resolve the troublesome issues of my life, and reorder all my relationships. However, I am reminded time and time again of the teachings of the Swiss psychiatrist, Carl Jung, who declared that the mind may grasp a truth immediately, but the soul is the agricultural part of our being that grows and heals very slowly. It is another one of those Philippians 3:12 things that reminds me that the journey is a long one: *"Not that I have already attained all this or have already been made mature, but I press on to take hold of that for which Christ Jesus took hold of me."*

Occasionally I still find myself neglecting daily prayer. I get caught up in some activity and totally forget about my evening conversation with the Father. I also may forget to return a phone message or even neglect to check to see if there is one. I just am not a methodical person. I exercise in spurts. I practice my clarinet sporadically. I devour books in bunches, and then may not touch another for months. My emotional archetype is more the hare than the tortoise. However, I am committed not to stray away again. I have learned my lesson. Life works better; it feels more solid, more secure within the fold. I do not want to find myself running on empty ever again. There is too much to do - too much still to be done.

I easily resonate with the words written long-ago by John Newton: "I once was lost but now am found; was blind but now I see." . . . and often find myself singing the old spiritual, "It's not my brother or my sister, but it's *me*, O Lord, standing in the need of prayer."

1. *Moments with the Devotional Masters*, compiled by Frederick Ward Kates, The Upper Room, Nashville, TN, 1961

REFLECTIONS

We live in a mystery. No scientist has begun to explain how - out of nowhere and no time - Creation came into being. When I say, "nowhere" I do not mean empty space. I mean no *where*. There was no space to be empty. There was *nothing* - not even an emptiness. Space began to exist when the physical creation of the universe began. Albert Einstein has demonstrated that time and space are not stable realities in any sense that we can understand. They exist in order to sustain the physical world. This really is beyond our comprehension, because we are creatures bound to the time/space continuum.

All this is by way of saying that the spiritual world is the only lasting reality, and we are essentially spiritual beings - now enjoying a physical existence. However, we are so immersed in the physical that we lose our spiritual roots. As Paul said in 1 Corinthians 12:4, "There are a variety of gifts, but the same Spirit." Some people seem more readily in touch with their spiritual dimension. Still, I believe that dimension is essentially open to all of us, and should not be ignored. Back in the turbulent 70's a critic of the Church observed that the Church can no longer say, "Silver and gold have I none," as Peter did in the first century. However it also cannot say (as did Peter) "But what I have I give you. In the Name of Jesus Christ of Nazareth stand up and walk." (Acts 3:6) Perhaps we have substituted the pursuit of success for the pilgrimage of the soul; a preoccupation with things of the flesh for things of the spirit. Perhaps we have substituted a series of religious tenets for a relationship with God-in-Christ. In doing so we have sterilized our faith and relegated it to a lesser realm.

QUESTIONS FOR REFLECTION AND DISCUSSION

1. Have you ever had the experience of sensing a presence that was unseen and unheard?

2. Have you ever thought, or known, you experienced God's presence?

3. What does spirituality mean to you?

4. Are you in partnership with God, or does it feel more like a franchise?

5. Is your prayer life personal and meaningful or merely a habit?

6. Is you prayer life a conversation or a monologue?

7. What would you truly wish to accomplish, drawing from God's power?

SCRIPTURE REFERENCES

Genesis 3:8   The man and the woman heard the voice of the Lord God as he was walking in the garden in the cool of the day, and they hid from the Lord God among the trees of the garden.

Genesis 4:16   So Cain went out from the Lord's presence and lived in the land of Nod, east of Eden.

Exodus 3: 5-6   "Do not come any closer," God said. "Take off your sandals for the place on which you are standing is holy ground." Then he said, "I am the God of your father, the God of Abraham, the God of Isaac, and the God of Jacob." At this Moses hid his face for he was afraid to look at God.

Joshua 6:27 So the Lord was with Joshua and his fame was in all the land.

I Samuel 2:21 And the Lord was gracious to Hannah, she conceived and gave birth to three sons and two daughters. Meanwhile the boy Samuel grew up in the presence of the Lord.

Matthew 6:5-6 And when you pray you must not be like the hypocrites; for they love to stand and pray in the synagogues and the street corners, that they may be seen by men. Truly I say to you that they have received their reward. But when you pray, go into your room and shut the door and pray to your Father who is in secret, and your Father who sees in secret will reward you.

Matthew 21: 22 "If you believe, you will receive whatever you ask for in prayer."

Mark 1:35 Very early in the morning while it was still dark, Jesus got up, left the house, and went to a solitary place, where he prayed.

Mark 6:46 After leaving them he went up on a mountainside to pray.

Mark 14: 36 He said, "Abba, Father, for you all things are possible; remove this cup from me, yet, not what I want, but what you want."

Luke 6: 12 One of those days Jesus went out to a mountainside to pray, and spent the night praying to God.

Acts 3:3 They devoted themselves to the apostles' teaching, and to the fellowship, to the breaking of bread, and to prayer.

Acts 3:6   Then Peter said, "Silver or gold I do not have, but what I have I give you. In the name of Jesus Christ of Nazareth, walk."

Acts 17:28a   "For in him we live and move and have our being . . ."

Romans 12: 12   Be joyful in hope, patient in affliction, faithful in prayer.

I Corinthians 12:4   There are a variety of gifts but the same spirit.

Philippians 3: 12   Not that I have already obtained all this, or have already been made perfect, but press on to take hold of that for which Christ Jesus took hold of me.

Philippians 4: 13   I can do all things through the one who empowers me.

Colossians 4:2   Devote yourselves to prayer, being watchful and thankful.

I John 1: 8-10   If we claim to be without sin we deceive ourselves and the truth is not in us. If we confess our sins, he is faithful and just and will forgive us our sins and purify us from all unrighteousness. If we claim we have not sinned, we make him out to be a liar, and his word has no place in our lives.

9. For the Love of God

Sometimes a series of apparently unrelated events falls in place to create a new understanding of life. This lesson of my journey actually covered a lifetime of little activities.

I realize how fortunate I was as a child. The church my parents attended was the Jefferson Avenue Methodist Church in Detroit, Michigan. It was a loving church. Mother chose that because it was the closest to our home, and Dad often worked on Sundays. The earliest church memory I have was as a child of three. My mother took me to a large room filled with children my age, gathered in a circle on the floor. She introduced me to the teacher who sat me at her side on the carpet, told the children who I was, and then had us sing a song which - ever since - has been dear to my heart: "Jesus loves me, this I know, for the Bible tells me so." I had absolutely no idea who Jesus was or what the word "Bible" meant, but the very tone of the song told me I was loved and that this was a safe place for me to be.

I have always felt loved and safe in the church. I have always felt loved by, and safe with, God and Jesus. For a long time I never reflected upon that tacit belief. Still it was there nevertheless. Like the old hymn proclaims:

> How firm a foundation, ye saints of the Lord, is laid for your faith in his excellent word. What more can he say than to you he has said, to you who for refuge to Jesus have fled?

I was doubly fortunate because I never felt unloved by my mother, even when she had just cause to be - and was in fact - quite angry with me. I loved her dearly. Dad, even though he was somewhat distant emotionally. never was unkind in administering whatever punishment was my due. He never once lost his temper and roared or raged. He was always calm, fair, and forgiving. Whatever punishment was given seemed fair, and when it was over, it was over. Dad carried no grudge. Justice was done and we got on with our lives. I never feared him. I loved him, as well. I believe these factors supported my quiet trust in God's goodness and love, and caused me to pass over the many proclamations I was to hear in later years about the wrath and judgment of God. I suppose I just assumed that if God was upset with me, He would get over it. Jesus' representation of God as a loving, forgiving parent (Luke 15:11-32) was the model my life experience accepted and embraced.

This does not mean that I felt I had carte blanche to do whatever I pleased without fear of consequences. That did not happen around my house. It was never suggested in church or Sunday school. There were plenty of reasons to follow the rules.

All of this did not come into my consciousness until I was somewhere in my fifties and had been a minister for more than twenty years. I was preaching the funeral for a good friend whose minister I had been back in my Ann Arbor days. The church was packed. Rod had been that kind of a guy. People who knew him loved him, and took the time and the trouble to travel to bid him a final farewell.

As I looked over the motley collection of friends I recognized a brilliant psychiatrist who gave much of his time as a volunteer caring for the mentally ill. He had great compassion, but was also rather leery of traditional, organized religion. There were members and former members of the congregation of Rod and mine. I also recognized many who were from different congregations in the city: some very traditional, some very conservative. In the middle of my prepared remarks I suddenly felt compelled to make this statement: "In the seven years I was Rod's pastor we never once talked about his having been - or needing to be - saved. Perhaps to some this will seem strange. However it never occurred to either Rod or to me that the God he loved and lived with, and served so very joyously was someone from whose wrath or punishment he needed to be saved." I was aware that this flew in the face of much of conventional Christianity. Yet, there was no negative reaction, either during or after the service. Most people just nodded their agreement and that was the end of it.

This caused me to ponder again the fact that there appeared to be so much negativity in our faith. The "don'ts" and "shall nots" seemed to occupy most of the rhetoric and drown out many of the words of joy and hope. Yet most of the people I know actually looked unworried about any future judgment or punishment. The majority of those who talked about the need for salvation appeared to assume they have attained it, and it's only a matter of concern for others.

I recalled my studies on Martin Luther and Lutheranism from my seminary days. Luther seemed to be terribly troubled by guilt. He simply could not believe that the consequence of his sins could be removed by a priest. Finally he bypassed the church confessional and went directly to God-in-Christ. Justification by faith he called it, rediscovering Paul's declaration of the first century. In his initial liturgy for the newly reformed church, Luther threw out the collective prayer of confession, calling it a man-made instrument of the devil. Later, however, he reinserted it without fanfare. Like an alcoholic sneaking his bottle into the house, wanting to be unseen, Luther was addicted to his guilt, and needed to constantly confess his failings. We had studied what we could learn of Luther's early life. His father was viewed as an overbearing, demanding person. Perhaps this is what set Martin on his particular theological path, as my relationship with my parents guided me in mine. I liked Martin Luther. I liked his straight forward talk. He never equivocated. You always knew where he stood. I admired the power of his mind, his magnificent ability to synthesize ideas, and penetrate into the core of issues. But I had always felt somewhat sorry for him, as well. He never seemed comfortable with his God . . . or with himself, for that matter.

The same could be said for John Wesley, the founder of Methodism: Powerful mind, plain spoken on the important issues of life. He, too, never seemed quite at peace with his God. Fear seems to have been a strong motivating factor for him.

Calvin and Calvinism also focused upon the negative aspects of the Gospel. The great American Calvinistic preacher, Jonathan Edwards, is best known for his sermon, "Sinners In the Hands of an Angry God," in which he depicted people hanging over the open pit of Hell..

Protestants were not the only, or even the first, to focus on the negative aspects of Scripture. The early Roman Catholic Church, which was our common heritage, placed great emphasis upon the need for forgiveness in order to avoid the perils of the afterlife. Their concept of Purgatory proclaims that everyone must pay in some manner for their errors. As I studied the New Testament Scriptures I noticed that only Matthew claimed that Jesus' blood was shed on the cross for the forgiveness of sins (Matthew 26:27-29). Mark, which is considered to be the memoirs of Simon Peter does not include the phrase "*for the forgiveness of sins,*" in Jesus' institution of the Lord's Supper (Mark 14:24-25). Luke also omits that statement (Luke 22:20-21). John does not speak of the event at all, but includes the story of the foot washing instead (John 13:1-17). *The Didache*, which is thought to be the teaching of the Twelve, and represents the thinking of the Jerusalem Church, calls the event the Eucharist (the giving of thanks) and does not even suggest that it deals with sin.

All the main branches of our faith somehow fell into the negative dynamic of fear. I wondered how much this reflected the times and particular circumstances of those who formulated the doctrines. We *do* tend to reflect the moods which resonate within us. It is something of the old puzzle, "Is the glass half empty or half full?" The pessimist sees the first, while the optimist sees the latter. Is Christianity about escaping God's wrath or is it about responding to God's love? You really cannot have it both ways, you know.

I recalled earlier days, when my daughters were young and I so dearly wished to protect them from the dangers of the world. A part of me wanted to erect a wall around the house to keep them free from harm. I would have loved to be able to protect their feelings from the abuse of others. I would have done anything reasonable to see that they were germ free and accident free. Yet I realized that my role as a father was to equip them to deal with reality and the guide them in the journey toward maturity. The world can be a dangerous place. Nature can be dangerous. My little girls had to learn how to deal with the perils of living and that can only be learned through experience. I also had seen adults who had lived sheltered lives, and noted that they seemed very shallow - emotionally immature. If I were to let that happen to my daughters I would have failed them. They needed to learn respect for the perils. Respect and not fear. There is a world of difference in those two terms. One has positive connotations while the other is entirely negative.

I had to ask myself if God as a loving Father had not organized the world in precisely such a manner as to enable us to grow to total maturity: physical, mental, emotional, and spiritual. The very idea of free will demands variability. There *will* be accidents. There *will* be mistakes. There *will* be lawlessness. There *will* be abuse. There *will* be all those activities which now take place which generate chaos, confusion, and fear. Does it make sense that God, knowing we will err frequently and sometimes disastrously in our use of the free will *he has given us*, should punish us eternally for those errors? I think not. Although I must admit I have found some satisfaction in thinking of the likes of an Adolph Hitler doing a slow roast in Hell. It satisfies *my* need for revenge. I doubt, however, that it satisfies a loving God who calls us to forgive seventy times seven.

For some reason I recalled a wonderful European tour I had led many years earlier. On that tour we visited a tiny church in the village of Itter, Austria. The group I was leading spent a day there, as a break from the historical sights and great cathedrals. We stayed at a lovely castle in a setting that was absolutely breathtaking. As we ate our lunch on the veranda I kept expecting Julie Andrews to come strolling down the hillside singing "The hills are alive with the sound of music." Most of us could hardly wait to explore the village and follow the winding road up the mountain. As we left the castle we came to a lovely churchyard. The lawn was marvelously manicured and filled with well-cared-for graves. Each gravestone held a plastic-covered picture of the person resting therein. I had never seen anything like it! For some reason I was compelled to linger, reading the names and gazing at the pictures. Our nation was still in the throes of being a death-denying culture, hiding

106

the cemeteries and disguising them as parks. These people accepted death and openly cared for those who had passed from this life to eternal life. The church steeple towered above the yard, pointing to the heavens, proclaiming victory.

I liked it!   I *loved* it!!

Then we entered the church building itself, and my mood immediately changed. It was baroque: gaudy, gaudy, gaudy. I do not appreciate baroque. I prefer simplicity. Moreover, the entire room was cluttered by far too many trimmings. It looked as though they had put something shiny anyplace they could find a space. But - again - immediately - my mood was altered. I recalled the cemetery I had just visited, and the great love and devotion it had revealed by the same people who decorated this church interior. Then I recalled my brother's and my own actions when we were young boys, back in the final days of the Great Depression. Every time we went uptown we stopped at the five- and-ten cent store and bought something for our mother. We only had nickels and dimes and the gifts were not very good ones, but they came from the heart, and our mother knew this. She always accepted them graciously and displayed them in some prominent place, so we would know our gifts were appreciated. There is no doubt that we junked up the house in our childish attempt to please Mom. We did this not because we hoped to gain anything from the gift. We did it simply because we loved her and dearly appreciated all the things she did for us. We had a *need* to give, to show our love . . . nothing more . . . nothing less.

The people of this church undoubtedly had been born in the village, baptized in this church, confirmed in their faith in this church, married in this church, and had baptized their children in this church. Finally they were buried from within this church. This was their home and God was their loving parent. Surely what I was seeing was their clutter of love, their expression of appreciation and devotion to One who had cared for them through their lives, and would care for them throughout eternity. I sat in a pew and silently surveyed their display of love and quietly envied their simple, trusting devotion.

Much of that tour touched on the Reformation, Luther, and Calvin, as well as the great cathedrals of medieval Roman Catholicism. They all bespoke of the emphasis upon judgment, punishment, and the need to escape from God's wrath. Only in Itter had there been the focus upon love and devotion.

All those events seem quite unrelated, perhaps. They fell in place for me years later after I watched a wonderful movie, *Chariots of Fire*. It was based upon a true account of two Brits who qualified for the 1920 Olympics. One was a Scotsman, called to the mission field, but also intensely committed to training for his Olympic event. His sister wished him to cease his training and concentrate upon his preparation for the mission field. His response struck some resonant chord within me. This was the final piece needed to radically redefine my understanding of the doctrine of salvation by faith. He said, "I know that God has called me to the mission field, and I shall go. But God has also made me fast, and I believe it pleases him to watch me run."

One of my daughters was a cross country runner. I loved to watch her run, not from a sense of fatherly pride, but from the sheer joy of sensing her exuberance as she sped through the fields and raced up the hills, propelled by her marvelous gift of youth.

This triggered me to thinking about what Jesus stated in Matthew 25:40 that "whatever you did for the least of these my brethren you did for me." This suggests that God actually does experience the relief and joy of those for whom we have cared. Conversely, as Jesus is quoted in Matthew 25: 45, when we fail to meet the needs and to ease the suffering of others, God also experiences their pain and rejection. I recalled the early church debates about whether or not God could suffer. Those who held to the totally transcendent God of Greek philosophy denied this possibility. Those who retained something of the Jewish God believed it possible. Again, my mind turned to the prodigal son parable and watched the father waiting for his son's return. I imagined the anxiety and the unabashed joy he felt. As a father, myself, this was easy to understand (undoubtedly why Jesus used that model). I have three daughters whom I love dearly. When their lives go well I feel a quiet on-going joy. When they are hurt, I hurt. When they would squabble in their younger days, I felt their anger and it upset me. If one was being abused I felt that one's anger, frustration and pain, and wanted it to stop, for her sake . . . and for mine. When they played well together I felt their harmony and their joy and experienced a gentle pleasure in just knowing that all was well with them and between them.

Perhaps, I thought, this is the real reason - the only reason - for us to behave as Christians are told to behave. It's not to escape punishment or to win rewards (stars in our crowns and all that). Rather, like my brother and I in younger days, or the people of that little church in Itter, we bring whatever we have that seems good and pleasing to our loving parent, simply as an act of love. If God experiences my anger, my greed, my callous disregard for others that is not what I want to give of myself to One I love so deeply. I would rather give my better self, not to win affection or praise, but simply because that is the gift of myself I would rather that God experience.

I am well aware that misdeeds have a way of coming back in painful ways. I also have a responsibility to society and to those dependant upon my actions. These considerations still factor into any moral/ethical decision. However, fear of God simply is not in my equation. It never has been. It never will be. *Love* of God does. Lest anyone think this is unbiblical, I would cite from I John 4: 18 *There is no fear in love. But mature love drives out fear, because fear has to do with punishment. The one who fears is not made mature in love.*

Is this not the genuine underlying message of Jesus? True, he also spoke in terms of judgment and punishment. That is the most primitive and least mature reason for being obedient. It is the kind of message that even young children can understand. However, Jesus also tried to elevate our thinking with such parables as the Prodigal Son, the Good Samaritan (Luke 10:30-37), the Lost Sheep (Luke 15:3-7), and the Rich Man and Lazarus (Luke 16:19-31). Certainly there are eternal consequences for anyone who turns away from God. I have to believe, though, that these consequences are self-induced, not divinely administered. We may drift so far from God and godliness that our souls are lost somewhere in eternity. But Jesus' model of God as the waiting Father tells me that this would be God's loss as well as our own, and it is not a punishment God would levy on *any* of his children.

With this understanding, Jesus has become even more important to me as a savior. I do not perceive him as one who came to save me from God's wrath. Rather, I see him as one who helps to save me from myself. In this regard he is a model and a resource to draw upon when my own wisdom and/or strength fails. He *is* the way and the truth and the life, as he was quoted as saying in John 14:6. When my will differs from His I know I am going astray. When I search for strength to do what needs to be done, He reminds me of the inner power of the spirit which is readily available if I but call upon it. As Paul said, *"I can do all things through the one who empowers me."* Philippians 4:13. When I fail and fail again, I am reminded of His admonition about forgiving seventy times seven (Matthew 18:22) and learn to have patience with myself . . . and with others as we struggle toward spiritual wholeness.

Our New Testament Scriptures teem with Good News, I see no reason to fear. Perhaps that first declaration by the angel to the shepherds sums it up best:

Fear not, I bring you good news of great joy that will be for all people.

Reflections

Clergy who still proclaim a doctrine of atonement today tend to contradict themselves. One moment they profess God's unconditional love. The next moment they explain the atonement as the essential condition for God's forgiveness. The Eastern Church never formulated or accepted a doctrine of atonement. They focused upon the Gospels of Mark and John which lack any hint of Christ's death being a sacrifice to appease a just and angry God. Their doctrine of Salvation could be summed up in the phrase, "The divine became human that the human might become divine." Actually, the earliest doctrine referencing Christ's death and resurrection was simply "Christus Victor." Many Christians sing it every Easter without noticing the implications:

"Love's redeeming work is done, Alleluia,
Fought the fight the battle won, Alleluia
Death in vain forbids him rise, Alleluia,
Christ has opened Paradise, Alleluia.
Lives again our glorious King, Alleluia,
Where, O Death, is now thy sting, Alleluia?
Made like him, like him we rise, Alleluia,
Ours the cross, the grave, the skies, Alleluia."

"Christ the Lord, is Risen Today" Charles Wesley, 1739

Thanatos (Death) was the enemy of humanity. It could not be defeated by mere mortals. When Death tried to claim Jesus, the Son of God, he could not hold him, and in rising from the dead, Christ broke the power of Death over humanity. Humans would still die, but they could no longer be held eternal captives. Charles Wesley incorporated this understanding in his great Easter hymn. Apparently he grasped the essential concept and chose to proclaim it as part of the Easter message. Although the philosophical concept of today has changed dramatically from that of the first century, the basic message remains valid: Death is not the final chapter in our personal history. The message proclaims news that is not only good; it is Great News! The implications are similar to those derived from the prevailing doctrine of atonement, but with entirely different implications: Our behavior does not determine a future reward or punishment. However, our behavior shapes our souls and prepares us for the next stage in a continuing journey. Jesus serves as the model for our behavior and our spiritual development. Paul states it well in Philippians 2:5-6, "Let the same mind be in you that was in Christ Jesus, who though he was in the form of God did not regard equality with God as something to be grasped." We are made in God's likeness, having been given free will. We may either attempt to create our own rules for living, or we may follow the rules established by God. Obedience draws us closer to God. Disobedience separates us. The judgment and consequence are self-imposed. Since we are free of condemnation, we are free to respond to God purely from love.

QUESTIONS FOR REFLECTION AND DISCUSSION

1. Were you taught to fear God's judgment?

2. What is your concept of heaven and hell?

3. Do you see God primarily as a judge or as a loving parent?

4. What is your motive for trying to be obedient to God's Word?

5. How would you explain Sin?

6. What does Salvation mean to you?

SCRIPTURE REFERENCES

Matthew 18:21-22 Then Peter came and said to him, "Lord, how many times shall I forgive my brother if he sins against me? Up to seven times?" Jesus answered, "I tell you not seven times but seventy-seven times."

Matthew 25:40 Whatever you did for the least of these brothers of mine, you did for me.

Matthew 26:27-29 Then he took the cup, gave thanks and offered it to them, saying, "Drink from it, all of you. This is my blood of the covenant which is poured out for many for the forgiveness of sins. I tell you I will not drink of the cup from now on until that day when I drink it anew with you in my Father's kingdom."

Mark 14:24-25 Then he took the cup, gave thanks and offered it to them, and they all drank from it. "This is my blood of the covenant which is poured out for many," he said to them. "I tell you I will not drink of the cup from now on until that day when I drink it anew with you in my Father's kingdom."

Luke 22: 20-22 In the same way, after supper he took the cup, saying, "This cup is the new covenant in my blood, which is poured out for you. But the hand of him who is going to betray me is with me on the table."

Luke 15:11-32 The story of the prodigal son.

John 14:6 Jesus said to him, "I am the way, and the truth , and the life. No one comes to the Father except through me."

Romans 12:1 Therefore, I urge you, brothers, in view of God's mercy, to offer your bodies as living sacrifices, holy and pleasing to God.

Philippians 4:13 I can do all things through the one who empowers me.

I John 4: 13-18 We know that we live in him and he in us, because he has given us his Spirit. and we have seen and testify that the Father has sent his Son to be the Savior of the world. If anyone acknowledges that Jesus is the Son of God, God lives in him and he in God. And so we know and rely on the love God has for us. God is love. Whoever lives in love lives in God, and God in him. In this way love is made complete among us in that we have confidence on the day of judgment, because in this world we are like him. There is no fear in love. But perfect love drives out fear, because fear has to do with punishment. The one who fears is not made perfect in love.

10. ANGELS UNAWARE

I think it was the wings that got me. The idea of winged people-like creatures flitting about just did not ring true with me. I assumed that angels were folklore characters who somehow found their way into Scriptures. They were not central to my faith. They were not even relevant. I assumed God could handle the details without them. So whenever I encountered an angel story in Scripture I discounted it and continued reading "the good stuff." At seminary we never even discussed the subject. That helped to confirm my unspoken belief that angels simply did not exist.

I was being "set up."

When I led a study group to Europe in the summer of 1970 I made a point of visiting Ravenna, the capital of the western Roman Empire from the fifth century until its collapse. The churches there have the most beautiful Byzantine mosaics in the western world. At the Basilica of San Apollinare Nouvo I noted the winged men standing by Jesus and quietly shook my head at their pious superstition. Then in the Basilica of San Vitale I saw the depiction of Abraham entertaining the angels unaware, as related in Genesis 18. Curiously these angels had no wings. They appeared to be ordinary men. "Ah ha," I thought, "That's why old Abe didn't recognize them. It was not his bad eyesight or the confusion of old age." Then a part of my mind began to question which depiction was correct: With or without wings.

While in Rome I made a point of visiting Ostia Antica. It once had been a thriving port city/resort, developed by Claudius as a gift to Nero. Then because of some poor political choices it had been abandoned in the fourth century, buried by the sands of time, and forgotten. Now it was being excavated and was a "must see" for any student of church history. While there I was startled to see a larger-than-life statue of an angel. "This was a pagan city," I thought. "What were they doing with angels?" Then it dawned on me! The word *angel* was from the Greek *angelos*, which translates as *messenger*. That angel was a messenger of the gods of Rome. Mythology had provided them with wings since they had no telephones and needed to get around in order to give their messages. When the pagan artists of Rome were asked to depict angels for the Christians, they quite naturally assumed they had wings. This is how they perceived angels. This undoubtedly is the way even the Christians of Rome perceived them. This is the way in which the entire Hellenistic culture in which Christianity developed understood angels.

"What if angels actually looked like ordinary people?" I asked myself.. That certainly would explain the differences in the empty tomb accounts of Mark and the others. Marks tells of a young man at the tomb, while the others tell of an angel - or angels. They all were *messengers*, were they not? I decided to take a closer look at the angel stories reported in Scripture. There were *dozens* of them. I wondered why I had never noticed that before. Then I decided it was simply because I had dismissed them from my mind even as I read them. Then I began to wonder if I - like Abraham - had ever entertained angels unaware of who they were.

Like I said, I was being "set up."

At first the accounts began to come in as second-hand stories. Then, they got closer to home. Two accounts came forth on the same evening. A couple we greatly enjoyed came over for dinner.(call them Ruth and Robert). They are well-educated and bright, with a strong faith, grounded in a theological understanding. Robert was barely seated before he began to tell his story. He had been to a school reunion, and had noticed one of his former classmates (call him Bill) who looked remarkably well-preserved and fit. His curiosity led him to enter into a conversation with him. Bill admitted his earlier life had been one of dissipation and capricious living. He even had suffered a major heart attack, and had been medically dead for a brief period of time. Robert said he eagerly asked him if he had seen a light or been in a tunnel. Bill replied that he had not experienced those things. However, he had been walking across a meadow. He knew that when he got to the end of the meadow he would be in heaven. He awoke in ICU with a plethora of tubes protruding from him. As he was recovering, a priest came to see him. Bill recounted his experience to him, and said he thought God was giving him a second chance. The priest replied, "God *has* given you a second chance, Bill. If you change your life, the next time you *will* be with God in heaven." Bill said he made a resolution to change his life, and had done so. As he departed the hospital Bill stopped by the desk to inquire about the chaplain. He had not seen him again, and he wanted to thank him. Bill was told there was no chaplain, and no priest they knew fit the description. Undaunted, Bill went to the nearest Roman Catholic church to inquire, and was told the same story. No priest in the area fit that description. He continued to check other churches, but always came up with the same response.

Robert finished his story, then paused, and we just stared at one another in reflective silence. While this was settling in and I was attempting to make sense of it, Ruth spoke up. "My turn," she said, then proceeded to tell *her* story. An aunt required surgery, and the family gathered at the hospital for the ordeal. Some time into the surgery a nurse, dressed in scrubs, entered the waiting room and said, "We're having trouble in the operating room. Would you all please pray?" She then turned and departed. The youngest son, who had slipped away from the faith stood up. "Let's all hold hands and pray," he ordered. The others did as directed. They prayed together for more than an hour. Then the surgeon entered the room smiling. "It was pretty touchy there for a bit, but your mother is going to make it," he said. One of the family thanked him for sending the nurse in. "I didn't send a nurse in. We don't do that sort of thing," he replied. "Are you certain?", someone inquired. "Absolutely! She would have broken scrub and could not return," was the reply. The family members looked at one another in wonder.

I respected and trusted Robert and Ruth. What they relayed was what they had heard, and what they believed had occurred. They were not trying to convince me of anything. They merely wished to share these remarkable stories which came directly from people they knew. We tried to make sense of these tales. Perhaps the priest in the earlier account was just passing through the area, and felt a desire to make a hospital visit. Perhaps the nurse was from another surgical unit who knew of the problem and contacted the family. She did say, "*We're* having trouble," though, and not "*They're* having trouble." Perhaps she used the collective *we* as part of the greater team. Whatever happened, Bill realized he had been given a chance to redeem his life, and he took advantage of it. And a young man who had lost his faith had it restored…and his mother lived. Coincidence? Perhaps. However, I once heard a quaint definition of coincidence: "Coincidence is God's way of remaining anonymous."

I was getting hooked!

Next, a member of my congregation shared this interesting account with me. Laura and her husband had been unable to conceive a child through their years of marriage. They decided to become foster parents to severely handicapped children. In this way, the absence of a child of their own could provide a loving family for some child greatly in need of that kind of care. We came to know them fairly well over the years. Our daughter, Crystal, who later taught special needs students served as a baby-sitter for them on occasion. One day, Laura told me she was standing in line at the bank, when a woman approached her and announced, "Honey, you are going to have a baby!" Laura was so startled that she said she gave no intelligible response at all. She did not tell her husband for fear of raising false hopes. About a month or so later, she told me the story. Why? You probably guessed it. She had learned that she, indeed, was pregnant. They moved shortly after the child was born. There is no spectacular ending. However, as I reflect upon it, I must ask why Laura had received this advance notice of what she would soon learn anyway. Was it to suggest that the faithful caring for the unwanted children of others was being rewarded? Was it to suggest that God was present in her life--that her life had a plan?

Then Cindy, another of my daughters, told me her story. She was hiking in Big Bend National Park in Texas. It was a very hot and arid day. She had neglected to take along sufficient water for the outing.

117

Somewhere, far from anywhere, she acknowledged her predicament. Cindy is a medical doctor. She *knew* that she was in serious trouble. She was dehydrating at a rapid pace. She was almost out of water, and was miles away from any help. She realized she very well might die there in the wilderness. She went down to the highway to walk back toward her camp. She had seen the highway from a distance many times that day, and had not seen a single vehicle on that road.

She plodded along, in a semi-daze, consciously putting one foot in front of the other to keep moving. Then a car approached her from behind. She had not heard it until it was almost upon her, and she feared it would pass her before she could even react. Unexpectedly, the car stopped and a young man called to her, "You need water!" It was not a question, but a statement of fact. He pitched a bottle of cool water to her, saying: "I'm through for the day, and don't need this." With that, he sped off into the distance. Cindy took the water like the children of Israel took the manna from heaven. It replenished her energy, and she made it back to her camp. That night she suffered the effects of dehydration. Still, she was alive, and would return to her children and to her work.

You may ask why the young man did not offer her a ride. I did. Cindy did not. He had done what was needed. He had given her water. She was alive. That was enough. Was he a heavenly messenger, or just somebody passing by? Who can say? Still, I must ask how he knew Cindy needed water. Was it an impulse? Why did he have cool water at the end of the day? Again, coincidence?

This angel thing was getting under my skin.

My wife, Diane, and I were winding up our week's stay at a condo timeshare. We decided to accept the invitation to take a real estate tour in exchange for two free rounds of golf. Actually, we were beginning to focus upon where we wanted to retire. The area was beautiful and this seemed a pleasant and profitable way to spend a few free hours. I fell in love with a prime lot just off the green of the first hole of the new, third nine-hole golf course. It was protected from any errant balls that might be hit our way, and overlooked a lovely pond set off by a background of beautiful foliage. "We can call it the 19th Hole!" I told Diane. It suited my quirky sense of humor perfectly. I envisioned myself strolling down the path to the first tee, playing a morning nine holes, then sitting in my yard watching the golfers go by. I even imagined myself getting to know them and calling each by name. We did not need to search elsewhere. This is where I wanted to spend those final golden years . . . by my own Golden Pond. I told Diane we would think it over then put a deposit on it before we departed. It was settled.

We played the gratis game later that afternoon. We loaded our cart then went to wait for our other twosome and the starting time. As we waited a pleasant looking fellow came by and inquired casually whether there might still be time for him to play. We wished him luck and continued our wait. As I recall, he was not a physically attractive person, still there was something about him which caused me to like him instantly. In a matter of minutes he reappeared and told us that our scheduled partners had not arrived, so he was to be our partner. His wife would ride along in the cart, but not play. We were about evenly matched and chatted as we played. Diane conversed with his wife and a good time was had by all. We concluded our game as the sun slipped behind the mountain and dusk fell rapidly. Still we lingered to talk a bit in the gathering darkness, because we were enjoying one another's company. He told me that he and his wife were scouting around to see where they might like to retire. He was torn between staying where he was comfortable and starting anew. I shared my plans to purchase a lot over on the next course. He responded by saying, "Dick, I believe that when a man has worked hard all his life he's entitled to the kind of retirement he wants." He paused, looked me directly in the eye, and asked, "Dick, is the this the kind of retirement you *really* want?"

I nearly hugged him. "No! No!" I silently shouted within myself. "This is a dream - a fantasy - nothing more. This might be ideal for many, but it is not what my life is about." I don't recall what I actually said to him by way of response. It probably was something to the effect of "Well I'm still thinking about it." Whatever it was it caused Diane to breathe a sigh of relief. She had wondered at my decision but always was supportive of me in following my dreams. Even if she had called me on this dream I doubt I would have heard her as clearly as I did this stranger who approached me so directly and unexpectedly.

I never saw him again. I have even forgotten his name. Still there was a quality about that encounter that lingers with me yet. I *needed* to hear that question. He came from out of nowhere really to ask it. Call it grace. Call it coincidence. It saved me from making a terrible mistake. A golfing, play-filled retirement is ideal for some people, but it is not what I was meant to do with the remainder of my life.

I was beginning to understand that this angel thing was more complex than I had imagined. Then the tables got turned. We were ending a marvelous month-long tour of the national parks. Only Grand Canyon remained on our list. After that we would stop off at Hoover Dam, see a show in Vegas, then fly home with a bag full of film and a lifetime of memories. We arrived at the southern rim in the early evening. As we walked along the edge peering into the darkening canyon I had a growing awareness that I *had* to hike into the canyon the next day. I even knew how far I had to go: four and a half miles. I looked at one of the many maps hanging about the area. If I took the Bright Angel Trail it would be about three miles to Indian Springs, the oasis dimly seen below. Another mile and a half on the trail would have me exactly . . . nowhere. I would be surrounded by rock and unable to see anything of value. However if I took the left branch of the trail as it left Indian Springs the mile and a half would lead me to a place overlooking the Colorado River. "That must be it!" I thought . . . Though I had no idea why I should want to view the river from there.

My problem now was to convince Diane that we should hike the canyon. We had hiked Bryce and Zion the days before. Those had been relatively short and easy hikes. Both those and the others, *e.g.* the Tetons, Yosemite, Sequoia held many things of interest along the way. Grand Canyon offered only barren rock and heat. Our original contract was to view the canyon from the rim, and then move on to Hoover Dam. Now for reasons I did not understand - and could not begin to explain - I felt the need to hike a total of nine miles into barren heat. I just presented it as one of those things I felt we should do, and suggested to Diane that she and our daughter, Crystal, could wait at the watering spot about half way to the springs. Diane was a good sport. She agreed to my plan, although it meant a boring two and a half hour wait in the small cave there.

We began our descent the next morning. It was actually quite pleasant . . . going down . . . in the morning coolness. We did notice that whenever anyone approached us climbing from below, we would smile and speak some word of greeting. They in turn would merely nod and maintain a stoic grimace. This led us to suspect that our return would be somewhat more difficult. Eventually I arrived at the springs. I swallowed as much water as possible, sensing the liquids being sucked from my body by the dry, hot air. Then I headed for the fork in the trail, planning to veer left. At the juncture, however, I experienced something quite unusual for me. For the life of me I could not get my feet to start down the path to the rim. I just stood there, feeling like an idiot, unable to make myself move. "Perhaps I need another drink of water," I told myself, so I went over to the pump for another swig, although I guarantee you I sloshed all the way. I kept telling myself that I had to get moving. It was going to be tight just making the hike as planned. Further delay would mean that Diane and Crystal would begin their ascent at the appointed time and I would make the entire journey solo. It was a prospect I did not relish.

Suddenly a young man emerged on the Bright Angel Trail. He appeared tired but agitated. "Have you seen a ranger?" he called to me. At his question I felt a calmness and an eerie sense of certainty that this was the reason I was here. "What's wrong?" I called back. "There's a man in real trouble about a mile and a half down the trail. He's cramped and can't even stand up. He looks like he's dying. My buddy is with him," he added. I told him to look for the ranger, and that I would go to help the man. Then I took off at the fastest pace I could muster.

I found the man sitting by the side of the trail. His heavy pack was still on his back, and the young man with him was just staring at him helplessly. I sent the young man on to Indian Springs to tell the people there I would bring the man along shortly. I removed the man's back pack and asked him if he had any water. He shook his head, so I gave

121

him a small drink of mine. As I talked with him I learned that he had taken the Kaibob Trail which has no water available. Also he had not eaten any breakfast. I gave him a small piece of a granola bar along with more water. Next I filled his canteen from the nearby stream and poured it gently over his head to cool him down. He informed me that his muscles were cramping, so I broke a salt tablet into quarters and gave him the smallest piece, along with more water. In due course he became more coherent, more energetic. I decided we should attempt the trip up to the springs. I donned his pack and supported his weight as we began the slow trek upward. I utilized the carrot and stick method, telling him of a shady spot ahead where we could rest and have some more water and granola. We would pause briefly at each resting place. His strength continued to return as we progressed along the trail. Finally we were able to enter into conversation. He taught Spanish at a public school in Wisconsin. In response to his query I told him I was a clergyman from Michigan. When he heard this he immediately asked me if I believed in angels. "Angels from the Greek *angelos*," I said (realizing it was the same in Spanish) originally meant messenger. Yes, I believe God sends messengers." His reaction to this was," I believe that today you are my angel." Now I have been called many things in my time. Even Diane in her sweetest, most supportive moments never thought of calling me an angel. I started to laugh it off - to dismiss his comment in some way - but I could not. "What am I doing here in this hot, barren canyon if, in some way I cannot begin to understand, I have not been called to be here?" I said nothing. I just silently nodded and kept trudging along.

As we neared Indian Springs he said to me, "I never thought I would live to see this place." I answered something to the effect of, "Well you did" (which was not one of my more profound retorts, but I was still mulling over his earlier words). At the springs others came over and offered to help him hike to the top in the early evening when it would be cooler. We looked at one another, knowing we would not meet again, yet sensing the bond which had been created between us. We just shook hands and said goodbye. I then turned and headed, as best I could, up the trail to try to catch Diane and Crystal. I knew it was about time for them to begin the scheduled assent - one and a half miles ahead of me. As I labored upward I ruminated over this angel phenomenon. "Perhaps," I thought, "we ourselves may be called to be God's messengers." This means we not only have to be open to the possibility that God has sent someone to assist us in our time of need, but we also must consider the possibility that God may choose us to become the messenger for someone else.

I caught up with Diane and Crystal about a hundred yards from the top.

Today if someone should inquire whether I believe in angels my answer is as certain as before. It is an entirely different answer, however. I realize I cannot prove that angels exist, just as I could not prove they did *not* exist earlier. It has always been a matter of faith, shaped by experience, examined by reason. If someone were to ask if I believe in heavenly angels - beings who transcend the limitations of mere mortals - I would answer in the affirmative. I would hastily add that I do not see them as equipped with wings, however. If someone were to ask if I believe in human angels - people selected by God to give a single message or perform a specific act - I would again reply in the affirmative. It seems to me that the trick is in knowing whether you are encountering an angel or just running into a stranger or friend with no particular insight. You also ought to be sensitive to whether God is calling you forth, or you are just being helpful. If someone were to ask me whether I believe angels visit us in other ways I would also give an affirmative response, but that is another step - another lesson.

REFLECTIONS

I do not subscribe to the theory that there are no coincidences, that *everything* happens for a reason. I believe there is a randomness to life. If that were not so then we are merely acting out scripts over which we have no control. Every action - every thought - would be predetermined.

There would be no freedom of the will. If that is the case, then our entire system of justice is mere sadism. People could not - or should not - be held accountable for actions over which they have no control. If every event is designed, then accidents do not just happen. They are programmed by outside forces. Then there would be no purpose in planning ahead, for what will be simply will be. No, there is a randomness, a freedom of the will, unforeseen circumstances which may - or may not - occur. Still, within this framework my life experiences have convinced me that there is a benevolent, guiding spirit which seeks to lead us in desired paths and to keep us safe from physical and spiritual harm. Some people may call it intuition which has caused them to veer from a dangerous path. I cannot distinguish from intuition and mere awareness of an inner feeling or thought. I have no idea of the source of an intuitive thought. I only know that I - as most others - have experienced them at one time or another. When I heed these inner voices, the situations I am in tend to work well. When I ignore them, I usually regret it in retrospect, and silently scold myself for having "gone against my hunches."

I also believe that most encounters have no specific purpose. They, too, are random events. They may be pleasant or unpleasant, depending upon the circumstances. Still, they serve no particular purpose and most encounters - and most people we meet - are forgotten. However, the Chinese proverb that "when the student is ready, the teacher appears," has merit for me. I would push the thought further, to say that "when there is a particular need, some one appears to fill that need," *if we are open to receive the proffered assistance.* Otherwise, the opportunity passes by with no awareness on our part that we have been offered - and have declined - some form of divine intervention. I also have to believe that these persons who appear in time of need may be ordinary mortals such as you and I, or they may be special in some way which defies description. I cannot believe that they are spirits which suddenly become embodied, but perhaps - just perhaps - they are persons whose very existence is designed to serve the purpose as messengers or agents of the divine spirit which Paul described as, "In whom we live and move and have our being." Acts 17:28

Questions for Reflection and Discussion

1. Have you encountered an angel along your journey?

2. Do you believe in angels?   If so, why? If not, why not?

3. Do you believe there are both heavenly and human angels?

4. Which, if any, of the related stories served to increase your belief in angels?

5. Have you ever served as an "angel" for someone? If so, when?

6. How would you have reacted to the various events told by the author?

Scriptural References

Genesis 18   Read in its entirety

Matthew 1:20 But just when he had resolved to do this an angel of the Lord appeared to him in a dream and said, "Joseph, son of David, do not be afraid to take Mary for your wife, because the child conceived in her is from the Holy Spirit."

Matthew 2:13 Now after they had left an angel of the Lord appeared to Joseph in a dream and said, "Get up, take the child and his mother, and flee to Egypt and stay there until I tell you; for Herod is about to search for the child to destroy him."

Mark 16:5-7 As they entered the tomb they saw a young man dressed in a white robe, sitting on the right side, and they were alarmed. But he said to them, "Do not be alarmed; you are looking for Jesus of Nazareth, who was crucified. He has been raised; he is not here. Look, there is the place where they laid him. But go tell his disciples and Peter that he is going ahead of you to Galilee. There you will see him just as he told you."

Acts 17:27-28 *So they would search for God, and perhaps grope for Him - though indeed He is not far from each one of us. For "in Him we live and move and have our being." as even some of His own prophets have said, "for we, too, are His offspring."*

Romans 8:28 *For we know that in all things God works for the good of those who love him and are called according to His purpose.*

Hebrews 13:2 *Do not neglect to show hospitality to strangers, for thereby some have entertained angels unawares.*

11. Ending the Masquerade

A new minister had moved into the area so I went out to greet him. I remembered when I was the new clergyperson in town, and had appreciated being shown around and made to feel at home. He was from a more conservative denomination than I, but I assumed that would not be an obstacle to our becoming friends - or at least cooperative colleagues. When I arrived at his parsonage he greeted me with a big "glad-to-see-you" smile. We stood in his doorway and chatted in a friendly manner, but he never invited me in, nor did he take me up on any of my various offers to meet socially or to share some cooperative efforts. Yet all the while - even as I departed - he had that "glad-to-see-you" smile on his face. I was to see him from time to time, but we never became close - or even connected. Still, I came to recognize the smile even before I could actually recognize the one wearing it.

One evening at a high school basketball game, this smiling minister took offense at a foul called by a referee. He suddenly rushed from the stands, grabbed the referee by his neck and began to shake him violently. Then, just as suddenly, he regained control of himself. "The smile" returned. He released the referee's neck from his grip, straightened his shirt which he had wrinkled, and patted him on the shoulder. "Just try to call them better, brother," he said cheerfully, and returned to his place in the stands as though this was a normal occurrence.

A year later we heard that his wife had run off with the Sunday school superintendent. His congregation was dismayed and could not understand why she would leave such a fine man.

That was my first encounter with a *mask*.

It was not to be my last. Shortly after this event a young lady began to attend our youth group. People commented about her beautiful, sweet smile. Personally I thought it was a bit too sweet. It reminded me of the too-good-to-be-true girls depicted occasionally in films who invariably revealed themselves to be anything but nice beneath their surface. Still, she seemed pleasant enough, became quite active, and I became better acquainted with her. She had lost her father at a young age and was desperately seeking a father substitute, and I seemed to have been selected. As she felt more comfortable in my presence her sweet smile faded and her latent anger began to ooze forth. It appeared to be a generalized anger, directed in part at her mother, in part at her lost father. She left for college shortly thereafter, and married a much older man about a year later. The last I saw her the smile was still in place.

I became sensitive to the masks many people wore. The most noticeable for me were some television evangelists who wore an "I-love-Jesus-send-money" smile. There were other public figures who also seemed to have set expressions, either of friendliness or profundity. For a while I was caught up in looking for masks, like a kid on vacation who looks for out-of-state licenses plates, to pass the time while riding.

There were many masks to count. Most were more flexible than the ones I described, but they were there. Some were just more observable than others.

As a clergyperson I was frequently used as a reference by parishioners and townspeople whom I knew. Every time I was asked to write a letter attesting to the character of someone, I realized just how little I knew about that person. We may have worked together on committees. We may have visited in one another's homes and attended many gatherings together. We may even have become close, personal friends. Yet, I asked myself, "What do I really know about who this person actually is beneath the surface?" So often I have been surprised to learn of some friend's - or some public figure's - misbehavior. Each appeared so squeaky clean, so honest . . . so teeming with integrity. Yet each was unexpectedly accused of thievery, lying . . . even manslaughter or murder. I had observed marriages which appeared to be ideal, something straight from the Donna Reed show, that erupted in messy divorces. Philosophers have forever been debating what they call the epistemological problem, which simply asks, "How do we know what we know? How do we know anything for certain?" Immanuel Kant observed that every so-called objective observation actually is, at best, a subjective opinion. We observe everything from the outside, and everything is filtered through the limitations and perspectives of our personal history. When we deal with people we almost always deal with their public personas, the faces they have chosen to present to the public.

One evening a bright, young minister from a neighboring church came as the visiting preacher during our Lenten series. I had heard many good things about him. He definitely was a rising star, destined for the great churches of our conference. We chatted for a while in my office prior to the evening's service. Although he was quite personable and obviously intelligent I had the distinct impression that I was in a dialogue with a slogan machine of some sort. His responses and statements came across like bumper sticker sayings, e.g. "We have to keep climbing!" "Life is a series of challenges which we can meet with faith." "We're called to fight the good fight no matter the cost." Later, at the moment he started to preach, he literally began talking out of the side of his mouth. I sat watching him in fascination. Then there began one of the strangest idiosyncratic habits I have ever observed in a speaker: A swelling appeared in his lower throat, rising up to his chin . . . followed by an eruption of sound somewhat akin to a gigantic belch. He seemed totally unaware that this had occurred and continued uninterrupted. I looked about and saw only an enrapt audience hanging on his every word . This "belching phenomenon" repeated itself at least a half dozen times during his sermon. Yet no one seemed to notice it. A few days after his visit I mentioned his name to various parishioners who had heard him just to see their reaction. I even observed that he had "an interesting delivery." Everyone responded enthusiastically, never even suggesting they had seen anything unusual.

This really confused me, and I even began to doubt what I had observed. Then I delved a bit deeper to explore different possibilities. Is it possible that we have some tacit agreement with one another that says, "I will not notice your mask if you do not notice mine?" Could

129

we all be playing a scene from the *Emperor's New Clothes*, pretending to see what others desire us to see . . . . caught in a web of self-deception? I had read about cultural blindness, and understood how we close our mind's eye to some of the unseemly occurrences. I had never before seen such a display of it however, and it staggered my mind.

Incidentally, years later, this young visiting minister, who had become a friend of mine, told of going through therapy "to get his act together." He now spoke in normal syntax and preached in a straightforward manner. He acknowledged that in his early days he had pretended to have a greater faith than he actually felt. The years and the therapy had helped him to draw his public persona into harmony with his true self. He could now "stomach" what he was saying and no longer talked out of the side of his mouth.

In one of my congregations there was a delightful, upbeat lady whom everyone seemed to enjoy. Perhaps she was a bit frivolous - even somewhat superficial - but it always was joyous and fun to be with her. As I came to know her I discovered a more serious person beneath that joyous exterior -or perhaps I should say - behind that funny mask. We discussed ideas and subjects that had substance and meaning. I learned that she actually was a very thoughtful, intelligent woman. She was not at all the cutesy, over-aged cheerleader she pretended to be. One day she shared with me that she longed for this kind of conversation with her long-term friends, who all were well-educated women. However, she said they simply would not accept her seriousness. When they first became friends she was still playing the role of a fun-loving bubble brain. She had long-ago outgrown that role and was weary of playing it, but her role in the group called for her to continue playing that assigned part. Her friends would not accept a change. So, in order to retain the friendships, she continued to don that mask and play her role.

Families as well as groups assign roles and demand compliance with the script. Actually roles serve useful purposes within families and societies. Most of us play a variety of roles, e.g. mother, father, sage, healer, leader. When they are appropriate and flexible they serve a purpose. The same can be said for masks. They may protect or reflect some portion of how we reasonably wish to project ourselves. In dysfunctional families members may play specific roles and wear masks in order to maintain some balance and to protect themselves. Dysfunctional families, for example, will have a hero, a scapegoat, and a lost child.. The hero becomes the overachiever who rises above the level of the family. The scapegoat bears the symptoms of the family illness and becomes the focal point for their anger and/or their illness. The lost child hides in the shadows to keep from being hurt. But - functional or dysfunctional - years after having left the family, many of us remain trapped in outdated, unsuitable roles, or wearing ill-fitting, inappropriate masks . . . without even realizing we are doing so.

At seminary I did my honors concentration in pastoral psychology. It was there that I reencountered the work of the Swiss psychologist Carl Jung. Somewhere in those studies I began to learn about the *persona*, the personality we present to the public. Its name, *persona*, comes directly from the word used to describe the masks which actors wore to portray the character they played in Greek theater. Per-sona means to sound or speak through. Immediately the word *hypocrite* came to mind. This was the technical term used for an actor in Greek drama. In time it picked up the connotation of someone who pretended to be what he was not. I recalled that Jesus was forever calling the good people of his time "hypocrites." He could see through their facades to perceive who they were without their masks. He often used the term in the technical sense as for those who are acting for public consumption. In Matthew 6:2, for example, Jesus says: *"Thus when you give alms sound no trumpet before you as the hypocrites do in the synagogues and the streets that they might receive the praises of men. Truly I say they have received their reward."* Again, in Matthew 6:5 he says: *"And when you pray you must not be like the hypocrites, for they love to stand in the synagogues and at the street corners that they may be seen by men. Truly I say to you that they have received their rewards."* Jesus was speaking of people who actually were giving public performances. But he often used the word in the more popular sense as in Matthew 15:7: *"You hypocrites! Well did Isaiah prophesy of you when he said, 'This people honors me with their lips but their heart is far from me.'"*

I spent time attempting to put myself in the Pharisees' position. They really must have been confused by Jesus' condemnation. Those Pharisees may merely have been following customs which had been passed along to them by parents and what we now call "role models." They may have felt a sting of truth in some of his rebukes, but my guess is that most really saw nothing wrong in what they were doing. Societies tend to tolerate and rationalize the many little corrupt practices which lurk beneath the surface of the gentle façades of its members, e.g. cheating on one's taxes, padding the expense account, taking "souvenirs" from hotels, or bringing home little bonuses from places of employment as compensation for the unrecognized work done. *Self*-deception: our own need to see ourselves in a good light, may well be the root cause of most hypocrisy.

Then I had this terrible realization: I *was* in the Pharisee's position! I was as much a hypocrite as they! I recalled reading in a long-forgotten book that only the unsophisticated, unreflective thinker believes he or she perceives reality as it really is. Then I thought of that old church joke of the story of the Pharisee and the tax collector from Luke 18:10-13:

Two men went into the Temple to pray. One was a Pharisee and the other a tax collector. The Pharisee stood and prayed thus with himself, 'God, I thank Thee that I am not like other men, extortionists, unjust, adulterers, or even like this tax collector. I fast twice a week, I give tithes of all that I get.' But the tax collector stood far off and would not even lift his eyes toward heaven, 'God, be merciful to me, a sinner.' I tell you that this man went down to his house justified rather than the other. For every one who exalts himself will be humbled but he who humbles himself will be exalted.

A Sunday school teacher told her class of the Pharisee who gave thanks to God that he was not a sinner like the tax collector who was standing at the rear of the synagogue. Then she told of the tax collector's prayer for forgiveness. At the end of the class, the teacher led her students in a prayer . . . giving thanks that *they* were not like the Pharisee. I had to chuckle at myself, realizing that whenever I had heard that tired joke I always gave a silent prayer of thanks for not being like that teacher.

Have you ever observed how much easier it is to critically examine others than to take a long, honest look at yourself? Yet, I have learned that the primary reason for reading Scripture is not to see how *others*

132

acted but to see ourselves in those *others*. We are both the prodigal child and the resentful older sibling. We are the uncaring Levite who crossed away from the beaten traveler on the Damascus road. We are the self-righteous workers in the vineyard who believe we should receive special treatment. If we fail to place ourselves in their positions, then I believe we misunderstand the meaning of Bible-based faith.

As I began to wrestle with this issue of self-examination, another situation developed which both sidetracked me and pushed me further into the process. A fellow clergyman had begun a romantic affair with a woman in his parish. She was single but he was not. Because we had become close colleagues in the rather small community, and because we were from different denominations, he chose to share this with me. Naturally I counseled him to break it off and attend to his marriage. Just as naturally he ignored my advice and continued the affair until it became public, and he lost both his marriage and his position as a minister. He soon left the community, married his lover, and began to pick up the broken pieces of his life. His denomination and his congregation completely abandoned him. Undoubtedly he deserved that treatment. Still, I reasoned that we Christians were supposed to be in the business of redeeming, not judging, so I continued the friendship. I did this partly that he might not feel or be completely abandoned, and partly to see if I could assist in helping him reassemble the pieces. I soon discerned that I was to receive more in learning than I was to offer in aid. It was *his* journey. I could only tag along. He had become completely estranged from his entire family: his children and grandchildren included. It mattered not what he did. The doors to their hearts were tightly closed. His only course of action was to begin to strip away the façade that had hidden him for years, and to try to build a new life on total honesty. I shall never forget his words, "Once you begin to take off the masks and discard the hypocrisies the task of living becomes much easier."

His new life did not appear easier. It was no better in most ways - more difficult in many ways - than the one he had abandoned. Yet he was determined to build this one on honesty, and to trust that with better roots the eventual fruit would be good . . . perhaps even godly.

"It's time - past time - really," I thought, "to examine my own masks and my own hypocrisy." To do this I had to journey backstage into the dressing room of my soul to see what roles I played, what masks I wore. It was an expedition I did not wish to make alone. The masks were so much a part of my being I was not at all sure I wanted to see what was behind them. Yet if they were to be removed I would necessarily find myself staring at the stark reality of myself. I did not suspect it would be anything so horrible as Dorian Gray's portrait. Still, I knew it would not be the image I was accustomed to seeing. It would not be so well-packaged . . . so acceptable. I would only make the journey if I could be accompanied by someone who really knew me - someone who loved me in spite of knowing me - someone who would accept the *me* I might have trouble accepting by myself. The words of an old spiritual began to play itself in my mind:

> *I want Jesus to walk with me.*
> *I want Jesus to walk with me.*
> *All along my pilgrim journey*
> *Lord, I want Jesus to walk with me.*

He who could call forgiveness down from the cross - He who offered forgiveness even before it was requested - He who could peer into the human soul and understand a person better than the person understood himself - *He* was to be my guide and companion.

Together we looked at some of my favorite roles. The Answer Man was a favorite of mine. Deep within my heart of hearts I had always wanted to know - to really understand - as much about creation as humanly possible . . . and then some. Somewhere along the way I had crossed the line and actually believed I knew far more than I did. I *wanted* to believe it. I wanted others to believe it. Not to know was some sort of failure. I also secretly relished the admiration expressed for my supposedly vast knowledge. Now in the moments of honest reflection I began to see the ridiculousness of playing that role. I remembered and laughed at the time I was traveling with a group of clergy when we spied a strange tower-like structure in an open field. All the others quickly admitted they had no idea what it was, and asked me if I knew. I rambled on for a few minutes with speculations as to its possible use, until I was interrupted by one of the group saying, "You're telling us that you don't know either, Dick?" I recall laughing from embarrassment. Now, upon reflection I could laugh at the absurdity of what I had done. And Jesus laughed with me. I recalled an evening meal at the parsonage with the entire family. Something had occurred that absolutely stamped my statement of fact as totally incorrect. My three daughters had gleefully jumped in to coach me: "Say it, Dad! Say it!" "I was wrah - wrahn - wrong" I replied. They all laughed and clapped their hands. Again I had laughed, partly to cover my embarrassment. This time I could laugh at the idiocy of the role I had chosen to hide myself from even my own family . . . And, again, Jesus laughed with me.

I began to accept the fact that I did not know a great many things, and was totally ignorant in some entire areas of knowledge. Then I encountered the marvelous book called *The Book of Heroic Failures*. Its dedication won my heart instantly:

To all who have written terrible books on how to be a success, I dedicate this terrible book on how it's perfectly all right to be incompetent for hours on end, because I am and so is everyone I know. 1

Say what you will but I believe my companion and guide led me to that book. It was precisely what I required to loosen that mask and free me up a bit. Oh I still play the teacher, the dispenser of knowledge. Now, however, I find it easier to say "I do not know." I find that the students often teach me, and I am more at ease in the classrooms. We shall always play certain roles of course. Living requires that we do. The problem is not in having roles, but in how we play them. How we wear those masks which go with our legitimate roles is the issue. If there are a variety of roles we play and masks we wear, and if they are flexible and honest, and do not mask the reality of who we are, then they serve a useful purpose.

Another mask of mine was that of social reformer. There was that idealistic part of myself that longed for the perfect world. I was prepared to take certain steps to help to make it so. Good sense told me to make my stands in a few significant areas for which I cared passionately. Somehow I became caught up in the role of the un-caped crusader. The

135

modest success I actually enjoyed attracted offers from other groups. I liked being sought after and *admired* (again that word). I joined every group that seemed to be worthy. I found myself heading committees whose goals were not particularly important to me, and writing letters I did not really mean. All this dissipated the genuine contributions I could have been making. It only served to bolster my public image and self-image as a *hero*. Eventually I realized that I had to stop playing this role and begin again to make *real* contributions. I removed the mask. I stopped performing that part. I selected the arenas which were meaningful to me and where I thought I might actually make some worthy contribution. I started to become a bit more genuine in who I was.

The list could go on and on. Some of the masks were more difficult to loosen. Some were much more painful, too painful even to relate. Again I would reiterate Paul's disclaimer in Philippians 3:12:

Not that I have already obtained this or am already complete, but I press on to make it my own because Christ Jesus has made me his own.

I would like to believe that the hands of my clock are rapidly moving toward some magical moment of midnight when the masquerade will end and all the masks will be removed. I have begun to suspect, however, that such a moment is reserved for eternity. The masquerade is ending, but it is not over. I still find myself using words to create a grander impression of who I actually am. I catch myself wearing the upbeat mask when my heart actually is heavy and I would dearly love to unburden on someone. However that self-image - and the image I wish to project - still clings to its mask. Some of the roles and masks are so much a part of my makeup that I have yet to discover them. I am vaguely aware that some portion of my hidden self probably is cowering in fear of discovery, and some portion is hiding from fear of being hurt. The masks which cover these inner selves are protective. They were donned in childhood, when I struggled with a speech difficulty and a terrible accompanying shyness. Others may try to mask feelings of inadequacy. A few are there to hide the shadow personality which lurks like Mr. Hyde somewhere beneath the surface. In this regard I am still learning the truth of what Jung said about the shadow being ninety percent gold. It just needs to be brought into the light and then can be transformed by love, which like the alchemist's stone can turn the basest of materials into something precious.

With a little help from my family and friends, the continuing presence of Jesus Christ as my companion and guide, and the ongoing grace of God, the unmasking continues. Without the masks I see more clearly. I breathe more easily. I am freer to address only those issues for which I feel genuine passion. And the interesting aspect is that my friends seem either not to notice - or not to care - that I look somehow different.

1 *The Book of Heroic Failures* by Stephen Pile, published by Futura Publications, London, 1979

REFLECTIONS

There is a difference between *playing* a role *and living* a role. Masks, however, are a different matter. They are worn with the intention of concealing - of deceiving. We have a variety of facial expressions that appear and change with the mood, the demands of the occasion. They actually should reveal what we are feeling or thinking at the moment. However, we are taught at an early age not to show some emotions, *e.g.* anger, fear, disappointment, so we quickly learn to don a mask of pleasure or stoic acceptance whenever we experience those emotions. We discover that these false faces protect us from embarrassment, criticism, or ridicule and learn to wear them with regularity. It becomes an easy matter then to select a few more in order to create the impression we desire. To this, we add roles which we play in order to win approval or gain some personal benefit. In one way or another we gradually become - like the Pharisees of old - hypocrites. We agree, or appear to agree, with others, when we actually differ strongly. We espouse ideas and causes that are actually of little interest to us in order to gain acceptance. We may even convince ourselves that what we say or do is genuine, which is the worst kind of deception By doing so we create our own little world which has little to do with reality , never aware of having done so. We become trapped in the illusionary world the Hindus refer to as *maya*. It is this illusionary world - generated by our egocentricity

- which binds us - and blinds us to the reality of the spiritual world which is the ultimate reality of our existence.

When an archetype first appears in our lives, we generally experience it by playing the role it calls for. Either consciously or unconsciously we imitate someone we associate with that role. It may be a teacher, a parent, a character from the media, or some admired friend. This is normal and healthy. However, in time, we should abandon the imitated role and assume one that fits who we are. I have observed young officers who act like some noted general, and young clergymen who sounded like Billy Graham when they entered the pulpit. Young girls often imitate their mothers when playing house. This may be amusing, but it is always acceptable. However, somewhere along the way the archetype should become assumed into the personality of the person. Otherwise there will always be something unnatural, something inauthentic, about what they do. They will have the smell of plastic about them.

QUESTIONS FOR REFLECTION AND DISCUSSION

1. Which masks have you observed worn by some of your friends or acquaintances?

2. Which masks in our society seem to be the most common?

3. Which masks appear most often on your own face? Which would you like to loosen?

4. What is the difference between a mask and a role?

5. What is the difference between playing a role and living a role?

6. What are some of the favorite roles you play?

7. In which roles do you find yourself stuck?

SCRIPTURAL REFERENCES

Matthew 6:2 Thus when you give alms sound no trumpet before you as the hypocrites do in the synagogues and the streets that they might receive the praises of men. Truly I say they have received their reward.

Matthew 6:5 And when you pray you must not be like the hypocrites, for they love to stand in the synagogues and at the street corners that they may be seen by men. Truly I say to you that they have received their rewards.

Matthew 11:28-30 Come to me all who labor and are heavy laden, and I will give you rest. Take my yoke upon you and learn from me, for I am gentle and lowly in heart, and you will find rest for your souls. For my yoke is easy and my burden is light.

Matthew 15:7: You hypocrites! Well did Isaiah prophesy of you when he said, "This people honors me with their lips but their heart is far from me."

Luke 18:10-13 Two men went into the Temple to pray. One was a Pharisee and the other a tax collector. The Pharisee stood and prayed thus with himself, "God, I thank Thee that I am not like other men, extortionists, unjust, adulterers, or even like this tax collector. I fast twice a week, I give tithes of all that I get." But the tax collector stood far off and would not even lift his eyes toward heaven, "God, be merciful to me, a sinner." I tell you that this man went down to his house justified rather than the other. For every one who exalts himself will be humbled but he who humbles himself will be exalted.

Philippians 3:12 Not that I have already obtained this or am already complete, but I press on to make it my own because Christ Jesus has made me his own.

12. FALL AND REDEMPTION

Our little daughter loved to dance. I believe she was dancing about the same time she was walking. Music would start. She would start. She loved it! We loved it! Everyone enjoyed watching her. She was graceful, but it was more than her litheness that entranced us. She danced with such wonderful freedom - like a young fawn prancing in a forest clearing - like a wood nymph floating in the breeze. I believe that in watching her we dimly recalled some moment when we ourselves were that free, and we rejoiced in that feeling.

One evening, at a church family party held in a member's home, the music began to play, and someone called for her to "dance for us!" Immediately that delightful little smile appeared, and she sprang into the small opening appropriate for dance. But in the moment that she paused to pick up the rhythm, she looked up and noticed all the people watching her. It was as though for the first time she was aware of their presence as she danced. I saw her shoulders sag, her eyes widen in fear, and her body droop forward. Although fully clothed, she crossed her arms as though to shield her nakedness, and slowly - so painfully slowly, it seemed - she walked off the wooden floor onto the carpet, into a corner, and quietly sat down in a large chair . . . still hiding her perceived nakedness with her arms. As she did this, I felt a subterranean sadness swell up within my being, and I said to a friend, "We have just witnessed *The Fall*, and it may take her a lifetime to be as free as she was just one minute ago."

Having uttered those words I had to examine them to understand their implications.

I had observed my other daughters' experience *The Fall*, but not so dramatically. I know that I, too, had gone through that same moment of loss somewhere back beyond the grasp of my memory. I vaguely recalled a seminary lecture on Lapsarianism, which dealt with *The Fall*. There were diverse schools of thought on the subject, called Infralapsarianism and Supra-infralapsarianism - or something like that (I don't think I ever got the titles straight). One school argued that God knew humanity would fall. The other said God planned for us to fall. It all seemed so abstract at the time, somewhat akin to wondering how many angels could stand on the head of a pin. In reflection, however, I had to wonder that no professor ever explained what that *fall* looked like - or felt like when it was individually and personally experienced. I think that is the key to this redemption thing we clergy are supposed to be dealing with. I think it is the underlying purpose of whatever spiritual pilgrimage we undertake: Fall and Redemption; Loss and Recovery; Separation and Return. That is the issue in a nutshell. Everything else is just methodology or trimming.

The story of the Fall which appears in Genesis did not just happen to Adam and Eve. It is every person's story. It occurs with what psychologists call *ego development*: the growth of the sense of self. We become the center of our own world, the focal point of all activities. Everything we experience is defined in its effect upon our personal life. During this period of development we are told what is acceptable about ourselves and what is not acceptable. We learn that there are parts of our personhood - things we do, say, or think - even parts of our bodies - which are not okay. We begin to don masks to conceal our nakedness, and veil pieces of our own being, even from our inner eyes. We do this in order not to see that which would prove painful, embarrassing, or less acceptable to God - to others and to ourselves. Like Adam trying to hide in the bushes, we sense ourselves separated, alienated . . . fragmented. Those parts of ourselves which we cannot accept, we attempt to hide from God, and hate them when we glimpse them in others. We find someone apart from ourselves to blame for everything that goes wrong, lest we perceive our own short comings and fail ourselves. Adam blamed Eve. Eve blamed the serpent. At some point in time this emerging sense of self blossoms into egocentricity. We - not God - become the center of our little world, and like Adam and Eve we discover ourselves somewhere east of Eden . . . outside the garden . . . lost and alone. We then spend the remainder of our lives longing and struggling to return home . . . to God . . . not even knowing what that may look like. Not even knowing where to look. (Genesis 3:24)

If anyone wishes to identify the nature of Original Sin, this is it. It is not some spiritual virus passed along sexually from generation to generation as Augustine imagined. It is not an accident of free will which thwarts the original intention of God. It is a God-given part of our human nature, designed by God to move us from spiritual infancy toward spiritual maturity. Those who would brand humanity as essentially sinners are wrong. We are made in the image of God. That is our biblical identity. We were placed upon this earth to fulfill that image. In the process we sin - or fall short - many times. I had heard it - and quoted it many times: "To err is human. To forgive is Divine." We were meant to err. It is the only way we really learn. That does not make us by nature *errors* anymore than sinning (falling short) makes us *sinners* by nature. Our nature is "Image of God." Sinning is something we *do*. It is the price we pay for acquiring wisdom and spiritual maturity in order to fulfill the image in which we are made.

Jesus constantly presented God primarily as a loving parent, not a judge, not a ruler. His image of the Prodigal Son and Waiting Father in Luke 15:11-32 is of a parent who wills our return. Jesus told that story to illustrate the will and nature of God. We all are prodigals who must move away as children in order to return as adults. I absolutely adored my children when they were tiny and totally dependent upon me. I readily admit that the teen years were trying times for everyone involved. Yet, now that my girls are mature young women, with families of their own, and rich in life experiences, I love them even more, and their love is more satisfying than when they were little children. I believe this is a small model of what God has planned for *His* children. Just as children (and their parents) must endure the terrible twos and teen years on their way to independent maturity, so this is a part of our spiritual path, as well. God has more than enough animals who act only from instinct. Humans are meant to be something other than that. We have been granted free will and given minds with which to reason our way along life's path. We are made in the image of God, and we are called to fulfill - to complete - that image in our lifetime. The early Church had adopted the understanding, "*The Divine became human that the human may become divine.*" Jesus Christ is our model "*He who has seen me has seen the Father,*" he said (John 14:9) "*Let that same mind be in you that was in Christ Jesus.*" (Philippians 2:5) The more Christ-like we become, the more genuinely mature we become. If we are not becoming Christ-like in our hearts and our actions, we may be getting older but we certainly are not maturing, and we have wasted our years.

As I look back upon my life it seems that every moral/ethical error, every sin, every trespass could be attributed to my egocentricity. Most of them very minor, but still failings. To the extent that I lived within *The Fall* I lived in fear and uncertainty. To the extent that I was able to rise up - or be raised up - I lived with more confidence - more love. This appeared to be true with everyone I knew, with everyone I had ever encountered. We have the moments of more severe separation and those high moments when we live more focused outside ourselves, more aware, more concerned for others. Having said this I must also acknowledge that not everyone seems to have suffered the same degree of fall. Perhaps it is a combination of innate personality and early life experiences which makes the difference. It is difficult to say, but we do seem to run along a continuum from mildly egocentric to narcissistic (a few saints, such as Sister Teresa, seem to have transcended egocentricity entirely). The road back is not so difficult for some. For others it seems nearly impossible.

There are some who will allow their egocentricity to dominate their souls. They eventually will evolve into narcissistic, sociopathic, or essentially evil personalities. They become capable of intentional destruction of all that is good. These are the ones who start wars, commit murder and rape, and plunder the property of others with no regard for the havoc they create. I need not spend any more time with this group, for I doubt that they would be numbered among the readers of this book.

To test my theory that egocentricity is the root cause of those ordinary little sins of commission and sins of omission which make up our daily lives, I began to sort through and examine the more obvious ones. The list was almost endless, but I shall share a few:

Driving is an ideal situation for sinning because of the anonymity and isolation it provides. Every traffic violation and every discourtesy rises from our egocentricity: DWI, speeding, reckless driving, running red lights or stop signs, failure to yield right-of-way, failure to signal before turning, and illegal parking all result from the preoccupation with the self that ignores the rights and well-being of others. When we rush ahead of a line and cut in, or fail to allow a waiting motorist to enter into our lane we do so from our self-ish-ness.

All marital and family strife can be traced to that same egocentricity, from actual physical and emotional abuse down to a failure to perform chores. Bad manners, failure to share or properly care for one another all stem from the same roots. Divorce occurs only when one or both parties has ignored the promise to "love, honor, and keep . . . for better or worse, for richer or poorer, in sickness and in health."

Poor performance in our work has the same root cause in most instances. We simply are more preoccupied with ourselves than with our tasks. We extend our rest breaks, day dream or chat rather than work up to speed. We overlook details we believe can be ignored, and are more concerned with climbing the ladder of success than performing the task assigned. If we are students we insist upon being entertained or let our minds wander during lectures. We may cheat and/or plagiarize to get better grades. Both bad teaching and parental interference are a part of the equation.

When we steer conversations to *our* points of interest, or emotionally sit on the sidelines we do so from egocentricity.

Egocentricity is quick to anger, slow to forgive. Everything is taken personally.

Impatience and prejudice are natural fruits of egocentricity.

Miserliness and hoarding are classic symptoms. Cheap tipping and retaining unneeded items rather than giving them to charity are examples of this failure.

Even when we act appropriately or charitably, when it is from a sense of obligation or guilt our motives are to avoid or assuage feelings of guilt rather than genuine concern for another. When our actions - no matter how noble or generous - produce an inner glow of goodness we probably performed more for our own purpose than for others. A line from T. S. Eliot's *Murder in the Cathedral* echoed hauntingly in my soul as I reflected upon this aspect:

> *The third temptation was the greatest of treasons.*
> *To do the right things for the wrong reasons.*

The realization that we are very much like those Pharisees of old came thundering back on me. Like them, we often do the right things for the wrong reasons. I recalled being in Ann Arbor, Michigan when Martin Luther King Jr. was assassinated. I had joined a hastily-organized citizen's group. We spent weeks discussing what could and could not be done, but we did little in actual fact. At the same time a group within my congregation began discussing the racial issue. Someone proposed we form a committee to study the issue. At this, an African American member said, with a sense of exasperation: "We don't need another study! We have been studied to death by well-meaning middle class whites. If you need a study, I can find one for you. What is needed is action!"

I began to see that all our committee meetings, discussions, and studies were but a means to assuage our own feelings of guilt. When the guilt had been sufficiently dissipated we would disband . . . possibly after making a few symbolic gestures. Our genuine concern had never been for equality. Our concern always had been for ourselves: our desire to feel good, or at least better, about our own privileged position.

As I reviewed the list, everything checked out. Most sinful acts are committed by nice people, decent people, who just happen to be so self-absorbed that they are oblivious to the sanctity, needs and rights of others The more we focus our world around ourselves, the more isolated and estranged we become. We then view the world as alien and unfriendly, and project the problem elsewhere. All the while we maintain our tiny circle of friends who in their fallen state support us in our distorted world view.

In the clash between Christ and Culture, too often, even for the pilgrims and the pious, Culture triumphs. Bigger is better and newer is nicer. We spend a great portion of our lives earning money, spending money, and collecting things. "Jesus said it well when he warned against storing up the earthly treasures instead of the heavenly ones (Matthew 6:19-20). Long ago I observed that people who seemed to be more attentive to others - less focused upon themselves - appeared to be the happiest. They might be lacking in possessions, but they were not lacking in what I believe Jesus meant by "treasures in heaven." What they did not have they did not seem to need.

As I reflected more deeply upon this understanding of fall and redemption I learned to interpret Jesus' words and actions differently. Scattered ideas began to fall neatly in place. Strange, the pieces were always there, but no one could put them together for me. I had to learn for myself, from my own life experiences. Jesus spoke in parables in order to make people think and discover for themselves the path he walked. He could not point it out. They would not understand or accept his way if it was handed to them. Time would alter the meaning of prosaic words, or people might not believe . . . not deep within their souls which is where faith and understanding must reside if they are to be of value. Answers obtained too easily are not as highly valued as lessons grasped from experience and reflection. Those come as *revelations* and are cherished as prizes.

I realized with a sense of sorrow that I had spent too much time as a preacher skimming the surface and never delving into the heart of our faith issues. But then, a person cannot lead others where he has not been, or to some place of which he is unaware. Perhaps that is how the term "elder" came into church vocabulary. Those who had traveled far enough along their pilgrim path to acquire a more fundamental grasp of faith issues were the ones the early church entrusted with its leadership. So what do we do? Are we doomed to wear masks, play roles, and forever remain somewhere east of Eden . . . longing for a home we might not even recognize until we are in it? Not at all! I believe I now understand something about the path and there are steps we can take which will set us and keep us on that path.

I have found reflective prayer to be an enormous help. I need a quiet time at the end of each day in which to review the significant activities of that day. Those events which either created accord or discord are the meaningful ones. There are usually a few - and sometimes there are many - to sort through. I find little value in traditional confessions. The early church had no such proscribed prayers. They called for prayers of adoration, thanksgiving, and intercession, but not for confession. That did not begin to occur until after the time of Augustine. These seem suited only for wallowing in self-pity or self-contempt. They also build in failure, because the worshippers know in advance that they will be admitting failure every time they worship. When studying the clarinet my professor instructed me to play each new number slowly enough to play it perfectly. "Do not rehearse your mistakes," he would tell me, when I attempted to play it too quickly. Generalized prayers of confession rehearse our mistakes. Let it be understood that my issue is not confession per se. Confession *is* good for the soul. It is the essential first step to genuine repentance. Scripture says it well:

If we say we have no sin, we deceive ourselves, and the truth is not in us. If we confess our sins he is faithful and just and will forgive our sins and cleanse us from all unrighteousness. (I John 1:8-9)

My issue is with ritualistic, generalized prayers of confession. They do not assist in our focusing upon the specific issues of life that are out of line. They are too much like the one-a-day vitamin pill or the all-purpose cleanser. I believe these, however, do more harm than good.

Reflective prayer is a different matter, however. In the quietness of the soul, we discuss with God those things that worked and those things which did not work. Then try to discern what made the difference, and how the failures might have been turned into victories. There is no use in blaming others. We cannot change them. We can only change ourselves, so let us work on that.

When I finally arrived at the point of examining the problem I had back at the military academy with the tactical officer, I had to confess that I could have changed the entire dynamic if I had not allowed my egocentricity to be in control. When he berated me for my messy room, I could have (should have) replied: "I am sorry sir. It will not happen again." That would have ended it, I am sure. Whether or not he was within his rights to admonish me in the manner he did, was irrelevant. I could not control what he did. I could only control my response . . . and I failed to do that.

I have attempted to incorporate that understanding in every awkward encounter. I try to remember that the person I am facing is a real-live child of God with good moments and bad moments, good qualities and some not-so-good qualities. My task is to see if I can elicit the good qualities. Sometimes I succeed. Sometimes I fail, allowing my egocentricity to dominate the scene.

Life is also made up of little victories for which we rejoice, give thanks, and attempt to understand. We need to incorporate and rehearse the good stuff as well as the lessons from the bad stuff into our lives. Our spiritual journey is as much a matter of remaining on the path as in returning to it. If there has been a particularly good moment, I examine the dynamics so that I might understand what I did that was right. I have learned it almost always was not so much a matter of *what I did* that was determinative, but *who I was* at that moment. Situations do not often repeat themselves, but dynamics do. We cannot plan what we will do or say for every possible situation. We can, however, plan on the manner in which we will respond. If that is in accord with God, then we will work out the words and deeds in a manner that is pleasing to God and unifying for all concerned.

Serious, reflective prayer is a first step. It must include time for God to respond, to question, to prod and probe, to keep us honest and on track .

Understandings are important. They can guide our actions. Words are important, as well, but they are intangible symbols. Actions are the realities which most profoundly shape our being and our becoming. Acting out our faith is step two. If we are to make progress on the path, we must "walk the walk." I named that portion of my journey which arose from my hospital clinical pastoral experience, "Learning to Love." It was by far the most profound experience from my entire seminary education. Away from words of the classroom and into the realm of suffering, struggles, sickness, and death: it became the reality which gave substance and understanding to all the words and ideas that had been bandied about in the seminary sanctuary. Caught in those sufferings one either eventually was stripped of self-concern or emotionally withdrew from the arena. When you interact with people who are caught in life and death struggles, desperately trying to return to wholeness, grieving for lost health and lost loved ones - if you have any unspoiled image of God within you - you *must* forget yourself and refocus your care and concern on those about you.

So many words of Jesus and Scripture had begun to fill my head during those days, each with new and practical meaning:

*For whoever would save his life will lose it, and whoever would lose his life for my sake will find it. (*Matthew 16:25)

Whoever would be first among you must be your servant. (Matthew 20:27)

And the King will answer them, "Truly I say to you in as much as you did it to one of the least of my brethren you did it to me. (Matthew 25: 40)

Why do you call me Lord, Lord, and not do what I tell you? (Luke 6:36)

Luke 15:11-32 *Read Entire Passage*

And a new commandment I give you, that you love one another; even as I have loved you, that you love one another. (John 13:34)

Beloved, let us love one another; for love is of God, and he who loves is born of God and knows God. (1 John 4:7)

I also began to notice the number of times Scripture speaks of Jesus having compassion, or of Jesus speaking of someone's compassion, e.g. Matthew 9:36, 14:14, 15:32, Luke 7:13, 10:33, 15:20 I still remember with tenderness some of those whose struggles I shared. It has helped deepen my understanding of the nature of Jesus: the very nature we are called to develop within ourselves.

I wish I could report that my growth from that total experience generated a straight line of progress, but I would be lying if I did so. Life continues to be a seesaw struggle between my egocentricity and the pull of God. It is by placing myself in situations which call for what Paul referred to as the higher gifts (I Corinthians 12:31) that the seesaw is most likely to tilt in the proper direction. In our better moments we can will ourselves to act in ways which will draw us from ourselves into the greater arena of faith. We can volunteer to assist where our help may be of value. This can range from visiting the infirm, working in a nursing home, becoming a Stephen minister, tutoring, assisting with a prison ministry, to leading a scout troop. It should involve interacting with people who have definite needs which they, themselves, cannot meet. Pray for them. Listen to them; weep with them when appropriate; and rejoice with them whenever possible. Eventually you *will* care for them. You *will* feel compassion for them. If you are unable to donate time, try money. Sponsor a child, family, or village in some emerging country. Pledge and give regularly, but also pray for those you sponsor. Eventually you will feel the kinship and humanity of those you sponsor. Now for the Catch 22 aspect: If you find yourself taking your spiritual pulse you will fail. Like the seed growing silently in Jesus parable (Mark 4:26-27) it will do so best without your attention. Your task is to sow it and nurture it. God's task is to allow it to bloom and produce fruit. If and when the fruit does appear, you will notice it and give thanks.

The third step follows quite naturally from the first two. The concern for self must be replaced by the love of God as the center of your being. Augustine has been quoted as saying, "Love God and do as you will." This undoubtedly is the best short course on theology that one can offer.

He meant that if you genuinely love God your natural desire will act in a manner to please God. Personally, I prefer Martin Luther's variation: "Love God and sin bravely." He was saying much the same thing, but acknowledging that we will continue to fall short in spite of our good intentions. His point is that we should continue to act out our lives, trying to please God, yet knowing that God's will is to redeem - to complete - not to punish or destroy if we fail.

It cannot be overlooked or dismissed by later theologians who would rather focus upon judgment and punishment. Paul's statement to the people of Corinth echoed in my mind, taking on new meaning: "*That is, in Christ God was reconciling the world to himself, not counting their trespasses against them and entrusting the message of reconciliation to us.*" (II Corinthians 5:19) Trespasses is a much more powerful word to me than sins. The Greek we translate as sin simply means failings - moral/ethical and otherwise. The term for trespass denotes an intentional crossing of the boundaries. Yet, Jesus and Paul both asserted that God understands, accepts, forgives and loves us even as we are.

I caution you to be careful about the form your love of God will take. I have witnessed many a pious lover of God whose love actually is a disguised form of narcissism. This is a subtle, but dangerous trap. There is some quality of being special to God lurking beneath the piety. The faithful saint feels especially beloved by God in return, and expects special treatment as a consequence of his or her devotion. At the risk of spoiling an old favorite hymn for the reader I must admit that I react against the last line of "In the Garden." It reads: "And the joys we share as we tarry there *none other* has ever known." (italics mine). This is just too exclusive for my taste. I would like to believe that *all others* have the same possibility, and that *many many others* have already known that particular joy.

To make the love of God your center is not so much a matter of adoration of God as it is incorporating God's love as your center. It is pushing you from the forefront and replacing that self-concern for concern for the greater community. It is loving your neighbor as you do yourself - not more - not less - but precisely as much. It is doing for others as you would want done to you - not from selfish desire, but from genuine respect and concern for all others.

How do we accomplish this? We do this partly through step two in which we act out concern for others until it becomes a natural attribute of our soul. Then partly back to prayer again. This time it is intercessory prayer.

Make a prayer list and pray for those on the list daily. List your friends who are having difficulties of any kind. Then add an acquaintance whom you barely know. Learn enough to know how to pray for that person. Include some public figures with whom you disagree. Do not pray that the person will change to abide by your will. Substitute God's will for your own and keep praying. Then include yourself in the equation to pray that you, too, might do God's will. Pray for those whose lives are in peril because of the acts of nature or humanity. When meeting someone, say a brief word of prayer for that person. Pray for those on the road with you in their separate cars. Pray for their safety and well-being. Pray for each member of your family . . . particularly the one who disturbs you the most. Pray for your enemies (It's biblical, you know [Matthew 5:44]). Paul suggests that we pray constantly (I Thessalonians 5:17). This may be impossible in today's society, but I still love the model presented by Tevyev in *Fiddler on the Roof.* Whenever there was an issue in his life he picked up his running conversation with God. This seems to me to be a reasonable way of fulfilling Paul's admonition to pray constantly.

This is the point at which I must pause. These steps I know, understand, believe and practice. One more time I hasten to repeat Paul's admission in Philippians 3:12:

Not that I have already obtained this or am already complete, but I press on to make it my own because Christ Jesus has made me his own.

I am certain, however, that I am farther along the path than in my earlier years. The buttons are more even. Life fits better. I am less apt to stray or become lost or confused. There is more feeling of wholeness within my being - more certainty of who I am and where I am heading.

I have stopped trying to hide, and live more comfortably within the spiritual dimension of my life - more comfortably in the presence of God. I feel more immersed in life, more connected . . . less alone. There still are fragmented parts of my being which call for reconciliation, of course. There are masks which cry out to be removed and roles which must be abandoned. Like everyone else I know, I still struggle with addictive behavior. But I feel I have moved to less damaging - even, in some cases - more helpful and productive addictions.

I hope these excerpts have been helpful to you in your journey. With Jesus Christ as my model and guide I continue the pilgrimage. I ask for your prayers. If you care to write me, I shall include you and your journey in mine.

REFLECTIONS

The Fall is a natural and healthy experience of being human. It may result in a disobedience to God. However, it should be viewed as a gift from God. Without it we would never have the opportunity to become fully human. If we are fortunate - and most of us are - we begin life as an innocent. We live in Eden. We are loved and cared for in our early years. We develop basic trust and a positive attitude toward people and life in general. At some point, however, we must leave Eden. We experience the power of the orphan archetype. It may be precipitated by the emergence of our ego, as in the case of my young daughter. It may arise as a response to a sense of abandonment or betrayal. When the orphan arrives within us we must depart from Eden. For a while we may simply wander emotionally, filling our days with activities, trying vainly to regain the sense of serenity we had experienced. I believe some people never progress beyond that stage. They spend their entire lives vaguely filling their days, doing their duty, perhaps, or simply putting in their time - at work and at home - always feeling a bit misplaced, never quite content with where they are or who they are. They seek relief in the diversions of life. Most, I believe, eventually experience the seeker archetype and begin some intentional journey toward the return to Eden. They may make many false starts. Our society certainly offers a vast variety of false goals to pursue. If their religious faith is valid and/or they encounter a worthy mentor along their way or if someday they wake up and realize their life has no worthy direction, they will finally seek and find a path that will lead them to spiritual wholeness. Most of this will be accomplished without a daily conscious awareness of being on a pilgrimage. Nevertheless, they are, and their lives take on new meaning and purpose. This may begin as a religious awakening that can be described as being "born again." However, it would be more fruitful for the convert to think of it as "reconceived." The gestation period is interminable - it is a life-long pursuit.

QUESTIONS FOR REFLECTION AND DISCUSSION

1. Do you accept the idea that the essence of sin is egocentricity? If so, why? If not, why not?

2. How did you react to the examples of daily little sins?

3. Which are most disturbing to you when you witness them in others? Why?

4. What do you think about the author's assertion that Original Sin is part of God's plan?

5. Do you believe that sin can evolve into evil, or is there some other cause?

6. How did you react to the author's criticism of the prayer of confession?

7. Have you tried, or are you willing to try, the three steps toward wholeness suggested? If so, how have - or will - you implement them?

SCRIPTURAL REFERENCES

*Genesis 3:24   He drove out the man, and at the east of the garden
            of Eden he placed the cherubim, and a flaming sword*

which turned every way, to guard the way to the tree of life.

Matthew 5:44. But I say to you love your enemies, and pray for those who persecute you.

Matthew 6: 19-21 Do not store up for yourselves treasures on earth, where moth and rust consume, and where thieves break in and steal: but store up for yourselves treasures in heaven, where neither moth nor rust consume and where thieves do not break in and steal. For where your treasure is there will your heart be also.

Matthew 9:36 When he saw the crowd he had compassion for them because they were harassed and helpless, like sheep without a shepherd.

Matthew 14:14 As he went ashore he saw a great throng; and had compassion on them and healed their sick.

Matthew 15:32 Then Jesus called his disciples to him, and said, "I have compassion for the crowd, for they have been with me now three days and have nothing to eat, and I am unwilling to send them away hungry, lest they faint on the way."

Matthew 16: 25 For whoever wants to save his life will lose it, but whoever loses his life for me will find it.

Matthew 20:27 And whoever wants to be first must be your servant - just as the Son of Man did not come to be served but to serve, and to give his life for many.

Matthew 25:46 Then they will go away to eternal punishment, but the righteous to eternal life.

Mark 4:26-27   And he said, "The Kingdom of God is as if a man should scatter seed upon the ground, and should sleep and rise night and day, and the seed should sprout and grow, and he knows not how."

Luke 6:36   Be merciful just as your Father is merciful.

Luke 7:13   And when the Lord saw her he had compassion on her and said to her, "Do not weep."

Luke10:33   But a Samaritan as he journeyed came to where he was; and when he saw him, he had compassion.

Luke 15:20.   And he arose and came to his father. But while he was yet at a distance his father saw him and had compassion, and ran and embraced him and kissed him.

John 13:34   A new command I give you: Love one another. As I have loved you, so you must love one another.

John 14: 9   Jesus answered, "Don't you know me, Phillip, even after I have been with you such a long time? Anyone who has seen me has seen the Father. How can you say, 'Show us the Father?'"

I Corinthians 12:31   But earnestly desire the higher gifts. And I shall show you a still more excellent way.

II Corinthians 5:19   That is in Christ God was reconciling the world to himself, not counting their trespasses against them and entrusting the message of reconciliation to us.

Philippians 2:5   Let the same mind be in you that was in Christ Jesus.

Philippians 3:12   Not that I have already obtained this or am already complete, but I press on to make it my own because Christ Jesus has made me his own.

I Thessalonians 5:17 Pray constantly.

James 4: 17 Anyone, then, who knows the right thing to do, and fails to do it, commits sin.

I John 1:8-9 If we say we have no sin, we deceive ourselves, and the truth is not in us. If we confess our sins he is faithful and just and will forgive our sins and cleanse us from all unrighteousness.

1 John 4:7 Dear friends, let us love one another, for love comes from God. Everyone who loves has been born of God and knows God.

1 John 4:18 There is no fear in love, but perfect love casts out fear.

Printed in the United States
50702LVS00006B/292-405